EASY WEIGHT LOSS • SATISFYING AND DELICIOUS

PLAY YOUR CARBS RIGHT!

**WIN THE WEIGHT LOSS GAME • TRUMP OTHER DIETS
SCORE CARBS AND DISCARD POUNDS**

- SIMPLE WEIGHT LOSS FORMULA
- OVER 200 SCRUMPTIOUS RECIPES
- 14 DAILY MENUS
- IMPROVES ENERGY AND OVERALL GOOD HEALTH

...WITH THE BRENNANS

ELLEN C. BRENNAN AND THEODORE M. BRENNAN
OF WORLD-FAMOUS
BRENNAN'S RESTAURANT IN NEW ORLEANS

OTHER BOOKS BY THE BRENNANS:

Breakfast at Brennan's® *and Dinner, Too*

SUGAR BUST FOR LIFE!… WITH THE BRENNANS
(also published as *SUGAR LESS FOR LIFE!…*
 WITH THE BRENNANS)

SUGAR BUST FOR LIFE!… WITH THE BRENNANS PART II

Published by Shamrock Publishing Inc.
P.O. Box 15439
New Orleans, Louisiana 70175-5439

Printed in the USA by

WIMMER
The Wimmer Companies
Memphis
1-800-548-2537

ISBN 0-9663519-3-2
Cover Design by Bridget R. Brennan
First Edition

Acknowledgments

To our son, Teddy, for his love and support.

❧

To our daughter, Alana for her time spent proofing and testing.

❧

To our daughter, Bridget—our collaborator and co-author. She was there every step of the way even giving this most recent book its clever name. How can we thank you enough?

❧

Our love and appreciation to all three of you!

Mom and Dad

Table of Contents

introduction

Thirty years have passed since we first learned that there was, actually, more than one way to lose weight. It was welcome news, yet hard to believe, that one could lose weight without starving to death. For us, then, as for millions of others now, low carbohydrate dieting was the answer to restrictive low calorie diets.

Caloric restricted diets had always been the one and only means to weight loss. Dietary plans of 700 to 1000 calories a day meant less than satisfying meals with snacks of carrot and celery sticks. Pangs of starvation prevailed and ultimate failure, oftentimes, loomed in the distance as a lifestyle of such deprivation was unrealistic to maintain.

Then, came an interesting, revolutionary, high protein concept which, in its purest form, was equally as unrealistic to maintain as any low calorie diet had been. A diet of only protein, mustard, mayonnaise and eight glasses of water a day, certainly, was a ticket for success but, surely, guaranteed failure and a serious need to dial "911."

To our rescue came what was simply called the "low carbohydrate diet;" possibly, a spin off of early, low carb diets, one rumored from the U. S. Air Force Academy and another, we recall, referred to as the "Drinking Man's Diet." The most appealing aspect of our new, low carbohydrate lifestyle was the prospect of losing weight while eating tasty, satisfying meals with even a cocktail or two. Only pocket size carbohydrate counters were necessary for implementation. We were unaware of any extensive testimony available supporting how or why this concept was a means for weight loss.

At this time, we were chunky newlyweds, having packed on significant pounds since our wedding day. We both worked at Brennan's Restaurant until very late at night and found only enough time to eat dinner after hours. By the way, we are not talking about a late evening supper of soup and salad. After a nightcap of J&B, we would feast on heaping plates of meatballs and spaghetti, steak Diane with potatoes

7

au gratin or fried chicken with corn and potato salad. We would retire for the evening immediately following a full blown repast totally exhausted and full as ticks.

A Mexican meal after midnight, once we had closed the restaurant on Saturdays, became a ritual. This, most probably, was our reward for working until the wee hours of the morning and for which our rotund figures evolved. To say the least, we could have written the book on how to lead an unhealthy, high carb lifestyle.

The purchase of our first carbohydrate gram counter ended our rapid course to self-destruct. This easy, little pocket guide, enabled us to implement a simple formula of carb counting to mitigate weight gain and realize success; indeed, this was the answer.

We were able to enjoy delicious, satisfying meals on our new, low carbohydrate diet. Meals were not only delicious but left us full and satisfied for hours. We learned quickly that dining out was easy and our social life was not in jeopardy.

We could still enjoy a cocktail if only mixed with water, soda or a diet drink. Unlike hard liquor containing "0" carbohydrates, a glass of wine or champagne did contain a fraction of a gram that required counting but minimally.

We had to admit that no meal, even a low carb meal, eaten immediately before bedtime would do anything but trigger weight gain. Once we eliminated late night dining and began counting carbs, we both began to discard unwanted pounds. We had learned to "play our carbs right."

Now, we would like to teach you how to play, too. We will deal you a dieter's Royal Flush, a winning hand of knowledge and experience. We will teach you the game of carb counting while feasting on delicious, satisfying meals. You will learn that eating correctly promotes weight loss and a healthful lifestyle. After all, the stakes are high, and we all want to be winners.

Why Count Your Carbs And Play Them Right?

Choosing the right diet can mean losing unwanted pounds and restoring good health. However, finding which diet is best for you is not always easy. Some dietary methods can prove difficult to understand and, therefore, seemingly impossible to implement. Low calorie diets for many are unrealistic to maintain for any considerable length of time. Low fat diets, actually, can cause obesity and disease as low fat, often, equates to high carbohydrate or high sugar content. Popular low fat diets, as well as any lifestyle rich in high carbohydrates and sugar, can pack on unwanted pounds and cause diabetes, immune system disorders, high cholesterol, high blood pressure, indigestion, adversely effect triglycerides while zapping energy.

Conversely, the litany of currently, popular, low carb diet books and the numerous compatible cookbooks espousing a low sugar, low carbohydrate lifestyle can remedy many adverse health problems. As the low carb craze allows significant quantities of protein in the daily diet, weight loss success, also, can be realized. Protein triggers a feeling of satisfaction for long periods of time and squelches the temptation to overindulge.

Nevertheless, not every diet is for everyone and what is successful for one person may not be for the next. We believe, however, for many people that a low carbohydrate lifestyle is most realistic to maintain over the long haul. It is not only a means to lose weight and keep it off but also a satisfying and healthy way of eating forever.

Today's low carbohydrate diets base their "why" and "how to" concepts on the theory that an individual's daily intake of carbohydrates, sugars and sugar equivalents needs to be decreased in order to lower blood sugar levels. The pancreas, then, produces less insulin triggering the body to burn stored fat for energy, resulting in weight loss and good health.

In various ways, each low carbohydrate diet embraces a spin on the best low carb road to success. A compatible premise is that a low carbohydrate lifestyle is not only a means to weight loss but, first and foremost, is a safe and healthful lifestyle to maintain. We concur that there are numerous health benefits as a result of daily carbohydrate restriction.

Our own personal experience supports the low carb theory which we espouse in *PLAY YOUR CARBS RIGHT!...WITH THE BRENNANS*. We write with firsthand knowledge of a low carbohydrate lifestyle without offering any medical advice. *PLAY YOUR CARBS RIGHT!...WITH THE BRENNANS* is not a medical guide and medical questions should be addressed to your physician. In addition, we strongly advise having a check-up before starting this or any other diet. Your physician, in many instances, can advise you regarding weight loss obstacles such as metabolic resistance, hypothyroid conditions, hormones or birth control pills.

Our reason for writing this book is to address the needs of all dieters who, for one reason or another, have not realized success or for those low carb dieters who are looking for an easier method than presently in place. Many low carb dieters have trouble defining moderation and portion control. They simply do not know just how much to eat and desperately need a specific formula.

We have combined our knowledge acquired through the years and our personal experience as dieters with an extensive understanding of today's low carb diet approaches. In doing so, we realized that many low carb dieters are merely looking for a simple method, easily understood and, therefore, easy to implement – a diet that cuts to the chase.

PLAY YOUR CARBS RIGHT!...WITH THE BRENNANS does just that. We demonstrate that low carb dieting is not boring nor are low carb meals monotonous. Our proven formula is simple, uncomplicated and will provide an easy, realistic means for living low carb, losing unwanted pounds and maintaining good health for a lifetime while feasting on scrumptious, satisfying meals.

How To Play Your Carbs Right!

Many of today's low carb diets can prove unsuccessful for two primary reasons. Either techniques are too complex to understand and implement or the lack of specificity in trial and error methods commonly spell disaster.

When weight loss slows down or stops completely and, in some cases, has never started to begin with, many dieters truly cannot determine the reason. Several low carb diets permit generous listings of acceptable, healthy foods for consumption; thus many dieters, inevitably, overindulge. Oftentimes, guidelines lack definitive limitations and fail to specifically state a dieter's boundaries; thus over consumption of even the "right" foods stymie weight loss.

An exact definition of just what portion control and moderation mean is necessary for those in need of clarification and direction. Without a specific formula restricting portions and defining moderation, understandably, many will just plain eat too much.

Keeping Score And Counting Carbs For Weight Loss:

First and foremost, your mind set must focus now on counting carbohydrates, not calories or fat grams. For many former low-cal and low-fat dieters, the adjustment might be a difficult one. It is important that you never allow caloric or fat content to discourage you from eating a food low in carbohydrates. Remember, it is your carb intake that is fundamental in losing weight, nothing more.

Weight loss should be realized by restricting carbohydrate consumption to 30 to 45 grams a day. Some people can lose weight consuming as many as 50 to 60 grams of carbohydrates daily; however, weight loss, most probably, will be slow. Keep in mind that you should lose weight quickly by eating foods with the least carbohydrate content or no carbohydrate content at all such as protein. Thus, you can control your rate of weight loss and diet at a pace that is right for you.

A reliable carbohydrate gram counter is essential, inclusive of food items from "soup to nuts" with brand names, ethnic favorites and fast foods, too. There are many to choose from either at bookstores or online. As time passes, you will be able to recall the carb content of many foods and will become less dependent on your gram counter.

Carb counting is easy as baked, boiled, broiled, grilled or steamed protein and fats are carbless; therefore, you need not refer to your gram counter at all! Throughout each day, even while dining out, keep a written, accurate accounting of everything you eat and drink when you eat and drink it. Just remember that every gram counts! What may appear to be insignificant carbohydrates such as meat, poultry or seafood covered in gravy, fried in flour or stuffed with just a few bread crumbs must be counted even if you add to your daily tally only a "guesstimate."

Most bottled, canned and packaged foods are labeled with a nutritional breakdown. This makes counting carbs easy and you less dependent on your gram counter. Still, be careful - the carb content on these labels is per serving only and, oftentimes, does not account for the entire item. In other words, you can't eat the whole thing unless the total carbs consumed does not exceed your daily allowance.

Every carbohydrate counts and even fractions add up. Beware of foods that are less than one carbohydrate. You must allow for them, too. In addition, be sure to include a fair guess of carbohydrates in herbs and seasonings. You will only cheat yourself in this hand of playing your carbs right if you fail to score yourself fairly.

Mini Gram Counter

Conscientiously, counting the carbohydrate content in foods consumed each day should result in weight loss. Be careful to pay attention to the size and quantity of all foods. For example, the carb content of a small apple is less than that of a large apple; therefore, precision is your only assurance to an accurate gram tally. Cautiously, estimate portion size and record gram count honestly. If you don't, you will only be cheating yourself. However, if in any one given day your total tally exceeds your daily allowance, do not quit! It is very easy, the next day, to compensate for overindulgence.

The following carbohydrate gram counter is a compilation of information predominantly found online. It is strictly for immediate reference to provide just a glimpse of what carb counting means. It is not meant as a substitute for the type of extensive gram counter available in bookstores or online. Whichever gram counter you choose should be your reliable reference for meals, snacks, grocery shopping and even dining out.

FOOD	AMOUNT	CARBS	FOOD	AMOUNT	CARBS
BEVERAGES			***NON-CARBONATED***		
ALCOHOLIC			Apple Juice-unsweetened	8 fl.oz.	29.0 g
Beer-light	12 fl.oz.	0.5 g	Chocolate Milk	8 fl.oz.	25.9 g
Beer-regular	12 fl.oz.	13 g	Coffee	6 fl.oz.	0.7 g
Bourbon	1 fl.oz.	0	Cranberry Juice	8 fl.oz.	36.5 g
Gin	1 fl.oz.	0	Egg Nog	8 fl.oz.	34.4 g
Red Wine	3.5 fl.oz.	0.2 g	Grape Juice-unsweetened	8 fl.oz.	37.9 g
Rum	1 fl.oz.	0	Hot Chocolate	8 fl.oz.	25.8 g
Scotch	1 fl.oz.	0	Orange Juice	8 fl.oz.	25.8 g
Vodka	1 fl.oz.	0	Pineapple Juice-unsweetened	8 fl.oz.	34.5 g
White Wine	3.5 fl.oz.	1 g	Prune Juice	8 fl.oz.	44.7 g
CARBONATED			Sports Drink	8 fl.oz.	15.2 g
Club Soda	12 fl.oz.	0	Tea	6 fl.oz.	0.5 g
Cola	12 fl.oz.	38.5 g	Tomato Juice	6 fl.oz.	7.7 g
Diet Cola	12 fl.oz.	0.4 g	Water	8 fl.oz.	0
Tonic Water	12 fl.oz.	32.2 g	Vegetable Juice Cocktail	6 fl.oz.	8.3 g

FOOD	AMOUNT	CARBS
BREADS AND OTHER BAKED GOODS		
Bagel	1	31.0 g
Blueberry Muffin	1	16.8 g
Biscuit	1	12.8 g
Bran Muffin	1	17.2 g
Bread Stick	1	20.3 g
Corn Muffin	1	17.0 g
Corn Bread	1 slice	13.1 g
Cracked Wheat Bread	1 slice	13.0 g
Danish Pastry, cheese	1	28.7 g
Danish Pastry, fruit	1	45.1 g
English Muffin	1	30.0 g
French Bread	1 slice	19.4 g
Pita Bread	1 pocket	20.6 g
Plain Muffin	1	16.9 g
Pumpernickel Bread	1 slice	17.0 g
Rye Bread	1 slice	13.0 g
Sourdough Bread	1 slice	12.0 g
White Bread	1 slice	12.6 g
Whole Wheat Bread	1 slice	13.8 g
BREAKFAST FOODS		
French Toast w/ butter	2 slices	36.1 g
Pancakes w/ butter and syrup	3	90.9 g
CANDY		
Caramel	1 oz.	21.5 g
Chewing Gum	1 stick	1.6 g
Chocolate, milk	1 oz.	15.9 g
Chocolate, semisweet	1 oz.	16.0 g
Gumdrops	1 oz.	25.0 g
Jelly Beans	1 oz.	26.1 g
Marshmallow	1 large	5.8 g
Mints, plain	1 oz.	25.1 g
Peanut brittle	1 oz.	22.7 g
COOKIES		
Brownie with nuts	1	10.1 g
Chocolate Chip	1	7.3 g
Gingersnaps	1	5.6 g
Oatmeal with raisins	1	9.6 g
Peanut Butter	1	7.0 g
Sugar	1	5.4 g
Vanilla Wafers	1	1.9 g

FOOD	AMOUNT	CARBS
CONDIMENTS		
Catsup	1 T.	4.1 g
Horseradish	1 t.	0.5 g
Jams	1 T.	14.0 g
Jellies	1 T.	12.7 g
Lemon Juice	1 T.	1.3 g.
Mayonnaise	1 T.	0.4 g
Mustard, brown	1 T.	0.8 g
Mustard, yellow	1 T.	1.0 g
Olives, black	5	1.4 g
Olives, green	5	0.3 g
Peanut Butter	1 T.	3.3 g
Pickles, dill	1	2.7 g
Pickles, sour	1	0.8 g
Pickles, sweet	1	11.1 g
Vinegar	1 T.	0.9 g
DAIRY PRODUCTS		
BUTTER		
Salted	1 t.	Trace
Whipped, salted	1 t.	0
CHESSES		
American	1 oz.	0.5 g
Blue	1 oz.	0.7 g
Brie	1 oz.	0.1 g
Cheddar	1 oz.	0.4 g
Cottage Cheese, creamed	1/2 c.	3.0 g
Cream Cheese	1 oz.	0.7 g
Feta	1 oz.	1.2 g
Gouda	1 oz.	0.6 g
Gruyère	1 oz.	0.1 g
Monterey Jack	1 oz.	0.2 g
Mozzarella	1 oz.	0.7 g
Neufchatel	1 oz.	0.8 g
Parmesan, grated	1 T.	0.2 g
Ricotta	1/2 c.	3.8 g
Romano, grated	1 T.	0.2 g
Roquefort	1 oz.	0.6 g
Swiss	1 oz.	1.0 g
CREAM		
Half-and-Half	2 T.	1.3 g
Heavy Cream	2 T.	0.8 g
Sour Cream	2 T.	1.2 g
Whipped Heavy Cream	1 c.	3.32 g

FOOD	AMOUNT	CARBS	FOOD	AMOUNT	CARBS
EGGS			**PUDDINGS**		
Egg, raw	1	0.6 g	Bread with raisins	1/2 c.	37.6 g
Egg substitute, frozen	1/4 c.	1.0 g	Chocolate	1/2 c.	33.4 g
Egg substitute, liquid	1/4 c.	3.0 g	Custard	1/2 c.	14.7 g
MARGARINE			Rice with raisins	1/2 c.	35.4 g
Soft and stick	2 t.	Trace	Tapioca	1/2 c.	14.1 g
MILK			Vanilla	1/2 c.	20.2 g
Buttermilk	8 fl.oz.	11.7 g			
Low-fat	8 fl.oz.	11.7 g	**FATS AND OILS**		
Skim	8 fl.oz.	11.9 g	All	1 T.	0
Whole	8 fl.oz.	11.4 g			
YOGURT			**FISH (uncooked)**		
Low-fat	1 c.	16.0 g	All	3 oz.	0
Low-fat, fruit-flavored	1 c.	42.3 g			
Non-fat	1 c.	17.4 g	**FRUITS**		
Whole-milk	1 c.	10.6 g	Apple	1	21.1 g
			Apricots	1	3.9 g
DESSERTS			Avocado	1/2	7.4 g
CAKES			Banana	1	26.7 g
Angel Food	1 slice	31.5 g	Blackberries	1 c.	18.4 g
Cheesecake	1 slice	24.3 g	Blueberries	1 c.	20.5 g
Coffee Cake	1 slice	37.7 g	Cantaloupe	1 c. cubes	13.4 g
Devil's Food	1 slice	40.2 g	Cherries, sour	1 c.	18.9 g
Fruitcake	1 slice	25.7 g	Cherries, sweet	1 c.	24.0 g
Gingerbread	1 slice	32.2 g	Cranberries	1 c.	12.0 g
Pound	1 slice	15.9 g	Dates	1	6.1 g
Sponge	1 slice	35.7 g	Figs	1	9.6 g
FROZEN DESSERTS			Grapefruit	1/2	9.5 g
Frozen yogurt, non-fat	1/2 c.	21.0 g	Grapes, American	1 c.	15.8 g
Frozen yogurt, regular	1/2 c.	24.0 g	Honeydew	1 c. cubes	15.6 g
Fruit Juice Bar	1	10.1 g	Kiwifruit	1	11.3 g
Ice Cream, vanilla	1/2 c.	16.0 g	Lemon	1/2	2.7 g
Sherbet, orange	1/2 c.	29.4 g	Lime	1/2	3.5 g
Tofutti	1/2 c.	22.4 g	Mango	1/2	17.6 g
PIES			Nectarine	1	16.0 g
Apple	1 slice	45.0 g	Orange	1	15.4 g
Banana Cream	1 slice	40.0 g	Papaya	1/2	14.9 g
Cherry	1 slice	45.3 g	Peach	1	9.7 g
Chocolate Cream	1 slice	29.5 g	Pear	1	25.1 g
Custard	1 slice	26.7 g	Pineapple	1 c. cubes	19.2 g
Lemon Meringue	1 slice	39.6 g	Plums	1	8.6 g
Pecan	1 slice	52.8 g	Prunes	1	5.3 g
Pumpkin	1 slice	27.9 g	Raisins	1/2 c.	57.7 g
Sweet Potato	1 slice	27.0 g	Raspberries	1 c.	14.2 g

FOOD	AMOUNT	CARBS	FOOD	AMOUNT	CARBS
Strawberries	1 c.	10.5 g	**MEATS AND FOWL (uncooked)**		
Tangerine	1	9.4 g	*BEEF*		
Watermelon	1c. cubes	11.5 g	Liver	3 oz. braised	3.0 g
			All Other Cuts	3 oz.	0
GRAINS			*GAME*		
Barley	1/2 c.	22.3 g	Deer (venison)	3 oz.	0
Bran, corn	1 T.	4.0 g	*LAMB*		
Bran, oat	1 T.	3.85 g	Liver	3 oz. braised	2.2 g
Bran, rice	1 T.	1.25g	All Other Cuts	3 oz.	0
Bran, wheat	1 T.	2.25 g	*LUNCH MEAT AND*		
Cornmeal	1/2 c.	46.2 g	*SAUSAGE*		
Corn Grits	1/2 c.	15.7 g	Bologna, beef	2 slices	0.4 g
Couscous	1/2 c.	20.9 g	Bratwurst	1 link	1.8 g
Rice, Brown	1/2 c.	23.0 g	Braunschweiger	2 oz.	1.8 g
Rice, White	1/2 c.	29.2 g	Corned Beef	2 slices	0
Rice, Wild	1/2 c.	17.5 g	Frankfurter, beef	1	0.8 g
Rye	1/2 c.	58.6 g	Frankfurter, chicken	1	3.1 g
Wheat Germ	1/2 c.	28.2 g	Frankfurter, turkey	1	0.7 g
			Ham	2 slices	1.8 g
HOT CEREALS			Pastrami, beef	2 slices	1.7 g
Cream of Wheat	3/4 c.	20.0 g	Pepperoni	10 slices	1.6 g
Oatmeal	3/4 c.	18.9 g	Salami, beef	2 slices	1.6 g
			Salami, pork	3 slices	0.9 g
LUNCH FOODS			Salami, turkey	2 slices	0.3 g
Fried Chicken Pieces	6 pcs.	15.5 g	Sausage, beef, smoked	1 link	1.0 g
Garden Salad	11/2 c.	6.7 g	Sausage, Italian, fresh	1 link	1.0 g
Pizza, cheese	1 slice	20.5 g	Turkey breast	2 slices	0
Pizza, pepperoni	1 slice	19.9 g	Turkey ham	2 slices	0.2 g
			PORK		
NUTS AND SEEDS			Bacon	3 slices	0.1 g
Almonds	1 oz.	5.8 g	Bacon, Canadian	2 slices	0.6 g
Coconut, raw	1 oz.	4.3 g	All Other Cuts	3 oz.	0
Macadamia Nuts	1 oz.	3.9 g.	*POULTRY*		
Mixed Nuts	1 oz.	7.2 g	All	3 oz.	0
Peanuts	1 oz.	6.0 g	*VEAL*		
Pecans	1 oz.	5.2 g	Liver	3 oz. braised	2.3 g
Pistachio Nuts	1 oz.	7.1 g	All Other Cuts	3 oz.	0
Pumpkin Seeds	1 oz.	5.1 g			
Sesame Seeds	1 T.	0.8 g	**PASTA**		
Sunflower Seeds	1 oz.	5.3 g	Macaroni, enriched	1 c.	39.7 g
Walnuts, black	1 oz.	3.4 g	Noodles, Egg, enriched	1 c.	39.7 g
Walnuts, English	1 oz.	5.2 g	Pasta, fresh	1 c.	34.9 g
			Spaghetti, enriched	1 c.	39.7 g
			Whole Wheat	1 c.	37.2 g

FOOD	AMOUNT	CARBS
SAUCES		
Barbecue, ready-to-serve	1 c.	16.0 g
Hot Pepper	1 t.	0.1 g
Soy, regular	1 T.	1.4 g
Tomato, canned	1 c.	17.6 g
Worcestershire	1 t.	0.9 g
SHELLFISH		
Clams, mixed species	20 small	4.6 g
Crabs	3 oz.	0
Crawfish	3 oz.	0
Lobster	3 oz. cooked	1.1 g
Mussels	3 oz. cooked	6.3 g
Oysters, raw	6 medium	3.3 g
Scallops, mixed species	3 oz.	2.0 g
Shrimp, mixed species	3 oz.	0
SIDE DISHES		
French Fries	20-25	29.3 g
Hush Puppies	5	34.9 g
Onion Rings	8-9	31.3 g
SNACKS		
Chips, corn	30	16.9 g
Chips, potato	10	10.4 g
Chips, tortilla	10	18.0 g
Crackers, butter flavored	4	9.4 g
Crackers, saltine	5	10.2 g
Melba Toast	3 pieces	12.0 g
Popcorn, unsalted	1 c.	4.6 g
Pretzels, salted	2 large	24.3 g
Rice Cakes	2	16.0 g
SOUPS (condensed)		
Beef broth or bouillon	1 c.	0.1 g
Black Bean	1 c. w/ water	19.8 g
Chicken broth or bouillon	1 c.	1.0 g
Chicken Noodle	1 c. w/ water	17.0 g
Chicken Rice	1 c. w/ water	13.0 g
Chicken Vegetable	1 c. w/ water	18.9 g
Crab	1 c. w/ water	10.3 g
Gazpacho	1 c. w/ water	0.8 g
Lentil	1 c. w/ water	20.2 g
Minestrone	1 c. w/ water	20.7 g

FOOD	AMOUNT	CARBS
Tomato	1 c. w/ water	16.6 g
Vegetable Beef	1 c. w/ water	8.0 g
Vegetarian Vegetable	1 c. w/ water	12.0 g
SUGARS & SWEETENERS		
Honey	1 T.	17.3 g
Molasses	2 T.	24.6 g
Sugar, brown	1 t.	2.9 g
Sugar, granulated	1 t.	4.0 g
Sugar, powdered	1 t.	2.5 g
Syrup, maple	1 T.	12.8 g
VEGETABLES		
Alfalfa Sprouts	1/2 c.	0.6 g
Artichoke Hearts	1/2 c.	9.4 g
Asparagus	1/2 c.	4.0 g
Bamboo Shoots	1 c. slices	4.2 g
Beans		
Black Beans	1/2 c.	20.4 g
Chick-peas	1/2 c.	27.1 g
Great northern beans	1/2 c.	18.6 g
Green peas	1/2 c.	12.5 g
Kidney Beans	1/2 c.	20.1 g
Lentils	1/2 c.	19.9 g
Lima Beans	1/2 c.	19.6 g
Navy Beans	1/2 c.	23.9 g
Pinto Beans	1/2 c.	21.8 g
Snap Beans	1/2 c.	4.9 g
Split Peas	1/2 c.	20.7 g
Broccoli	1/2 c.	4.0 g
Brussels Sprouts	1/2 c.	6.8 g
Cabbage, celery	1/2 c.	1.4 g
Cabbage, red	1/2 c.	3.5 g
Cabbage, savoy	1/2 c.	4.0 g
Carrot	1	7.3 g
Cauliflower	3 florets	2.8 g
Celery	1/2 c.	2.2 g
Chives	1 T.	0.1 g
Corn	Kernels of 1 ear	19.3 g
Cucumber	1/2	4.4 g
Eggplant	1/2 c.	3.2 g
Endive	1/2 c.	0.8 g

FOOD	AMOUNT	CARBS
Garlic	1 clove	1.0 g
Ginger Root	1 T.	0.9 g
Kale	1/2 c.	3.7 g
Leeks	1/2 c.	4.0 g
Lettuce, butterhead	1 c. shredded	1.0 g
Lettuce, iceberg	1 c. shredded	2.8 g
Lettuce, romaine	1 c. shredded	1.3 g
Mushrooms	1/2 c.	4.0 g
Onions	1/2 c.	6.9 g
Parsley	1/2 c.	2.1 g
Peppers, chili	1 T.	0.9 g
Peppers, green bell	1/2 c.	3.2 g
Peppers, red bell	1/2 c.	3.2 g
Potato	1	51.0
Pumpkin, canned	1/2 c.	9.9 g
Radishes	1/2 c.	2.0 g
Rhubarb	1/2 c.	2.75 g
Scallions	1/2 c.	3.7 g
Shallots	1 T.	1.7 g
Spinach	1/2 c.	3.4 g
Squash, acorn	1/2 c.	14.9 g
Squash, butternut	1/2 c.	10.7 g
Squash, crookneck/straightneck	1/2 c.	3.9 g
Squash, hubbard	1/2 c.	11.0 g
Squash, spaghetti	1/2 c.	5.0 g
Squash, zucchini	1/2 c.	3.5 g
Sweet Potato	1	27.7 g
Tomato	1	5.7 g
Turnips	1/2 c.	3.8 g
Watercress	1/2 c.	0.2 g
Yams	1/2 c.	18.7 g

NOTES:

Bonus Pointers

Our "Bonus Pointers" should help you make the right choices while maintaining a healthful lifestyle. Emphasis is given to fundamental dietary and nutritional information for total comprehension of a low carb concept. Guidance in technique and tips for weight loss success, also, are essential. Incorporating much of the following information into your lifestyle while you *PLAY YOUR CARBS RIGHT!...WITH THE BRENNANS* will expedite weight loss and affirm your road to good health.

Carbohydrates

As in any low carb diet, be aware of exactly which carbohydrates you should include in your daily regimen. The right low carb fruit and vegetables can provide important vitamins and may be your only source of fiber while dieting. Be wise in your choices. Leafy green salads, broccoli, cabbage, greens and spinach, to name a few, are all low carb and great sources of vitamins and fiber. For those hard to come by low carb fruit, cantaloupe, strawberries and peaches are a few choices that will easily fit within your daily gram allowance.

Beware of foods high in carbohydrates! Although many will not adversely affect weight loss, as long as your daily gram count does not exceed 30 to 45 grams, just know that they can be unhealthy.

Many food products labeled low fat and "healthy" such as diet and energy bars are, oftentimes, anything but healthy. They can be chocked full of sugar and sugar derivatives, such as honey that are equally as unhealthy as refined sugar; thus keeping people fat and prone to disease.

When grocery shopping, remember that fresh is always best. Frozen foods should be your second choice and canned foods your last as they are most likely to be packed in sugar, sugar derivatives, sodium, nitrates and other unhealthy preservatives. Whether losing weight or maintaining a healthy lifestyle, knowing how to read a label is essential.

Inspection of a food product does not end at reading the number of carb grams per serving to add to your daily gram tally. It is necessary as well to inspect the detailed list of ingredients, some of which can prove unhealthy and high in carbohydrates.

When reading a label, the following ingredients should denote caution:

Barley Malt	Honey
Beet Juice	Malted Barley
Beet Sugar	Maltodextrin
Brown Rice Syrup	Maltose
Brown Sugar	Maple Syrup
Cane Juice	Modified Food Starch
Cane Syrup	Modified Tapioca Starch
Cornstarch	Molasses
Corn Syrup	Raisin Juice
Dextrose	Potato Starch
Flour: Corn, Enriched Wheat and White	Sugar, Raw and Refined
Glucose	Sucrose
High Fructose Corn Syrup	

Protein

While essentially healthy, satiating and delicious, most protein is gramless! In other words, most types of protein such as meat, poultry and fish contain zero grams of carbohydrates. As most shellfish do contain small amounts of carbohydrates and certain proteins, such as cheese and eggs have fractional grams of carbs, careful counting is required. For this reason, never assume the carb content of a food without referring to your gram counter for accuracy. Every bit counts, even a fraction of a gram.

Weight loss can become an easy, quick reality while dining on satisfyingly, delicious meals of vitally important protein. Not only is protein most satisfying, but it also represses hunger pangs for long periods of time. Particularly, interesting is the fact that eating protein alone can expedite weight loss. Eating a piece of meat, chicken or seafood by itself without any other food group will signal the pancreas to secrete the enzyme glucagon which in turn breaks down stored, unwanted fat for use as energy.

Fats

Let's face it. Fat makes food taste good. Fat consumption is not only carbless, but the flavor and taste of most fats provide a sense of satisfaction not otherwise realized in low fat diets. Low carb dieters feel less deprived when fat is allowed in the preparation of sauces, salad dressings and other favorite foods. Variety and flavor displace the monotony of most diets and help the low carb dieter stay the course.

We all have been brain washed that, unequivocally, fats are unhealthy. Low fat diets became the craze that, inevitably, made many people fat and some, even, fatter. Obesity and diseases, such as diabetes, became the pitfalls of low fat dieting. The response to this restrictive low fat lifestyle has been the low carb craze of today.

We recognize that while fat consumption will not elevate your carb count for the day, it is important when making wise food choices to take into account that for overall good health, some fats are better to choose than others. Saturated fats can increase your blood cholesterol level or low-density lipoproteins (LDL), known as "bad" cholesterol.

On the other hand, monounsaturated fats, such as avocado, canola, nut, olive and fish oils can be good for you as they should not adversely affect your high-density lipoproteins (HDL) or "good" cholesterol and can actually elevate HDL levels. If given the option, try to choose monounsaturated fats over polyunsaturated and saturated fats. For example, it is recommended to choose canola and olive oil instead of butter. Also, it is always best to feast on lean cuts of meat and skinless chicken.

Fiber

Fiber is essential to good health but can be difficult to include in a low carb weight loss program. It is important to choose green, leafy vegetables and cruciferous ones such as broccoli, cabbage and cauliflower as well as fruit such as grapefruit or berries for the best natural sources of fiber. A dietary supplement of fiber found in health food stores is helpful during the low carb weight loss phase, when adequate servings of whole grains and other natural sources of fiber, usually, are prohibitive for daily carbohydrate allowances.

Water

Drinking at least eight 12 ounce glasses of water a day is very important for several reasons. First and foremost, water enhances the weight loss process, cleanses the body of toxic waste and remedies fluid retention. It is, especially, helpful to drink one or two glasses of water before breakfast to expedite these benefits. Water is essential to avoid dehydration for low carb dieters and, especially, for those who exercise as well. Drinking a large glass of cold water before any meal can reduce hunger so that you will eat less food.

Caffeine

Coffee, tea, many sugar free beverages and certain foods, such as chocolate, contain significant amounts of caffeine. They all may be consumed in moderation, but exercise caution as caffeine can stimulate your appetite.

Sodium

Limiting your sodium intake is, also, important as sodium can cause fluid retention and high blood pressure. Drinking an adequate amount of water helps to eliminate excess sodium from your body. Be wary of some sugar free beverages that are high in sodium content.

Vitamins

We are firm believers in vitamin, mineral and other nutritional supplements whether dieting or not. These supplements are crucial to combat aging and disease. Unfortunately, most people do not obtain adequate vitamins, essential for good health, from their daily intake of food. Alcohol and caffeine consumption can cause vitamin and mineral depletion; elements in our environment and other factors in our lifestyles can cause deficiencies as well.

We could go on and on with what we believe is necessary to maintain good health through proper vitamin and nutritional supplementation. However, suffice it to say that most any diet does not adequately derive essential vitamins and minerals from the foods consumed.

In order to compensate for most deficiencies, particularly present in a weight loss regimen, we highly recommend a good multi-purpose vitamin, in addition to some form of fiber supplement. Vitamins A, B, C, D, E as well as calcium, magnesium, potassium, selenium and zinc are important. The composition of any supplement should never contain sugar or starch; and when counting carbs read the bottle or package label just as you would any food item. In addition, be sure to do the same with any over the counter medication.

Exercise

Exercise is important for cardiovascular fitness and your overall health. Exercise, also, should increase your rate of metabolism that, in turn, can expedite weight loss. Many people may choose to exercise first thing in the morning. However, there are those who believe that exercising after dinner proves most beneficial. Of course, it goes without saying, check with your physician as to the best type of exercise for you.

Alcohol

Alcoholic beverages should not interfere with weight loss although they may slow down the process to some degree; alcohol can inhibit any diet. First and foremost, alcohol is an appetite stimulant. We suggest that you never drink alcohol on an empty stomach; and moderation should be exercised even when the carbohydrate grams do not exceed your daily allowance.

Be sure that mixed drinks include water, soda or any sugar free beverage unless the mixer does not exceed your daily carb limit. Don't forget that those lemons, limes and edible garnish count, too!

Beware of most beers! Unlike hard liquor, they are extremely high in carbohydrates. However, light beer, usually, has a reasonable carb content.

Red wine is not only low in carbs but drinking a glass of red wine daily, actually, can benefit your cardiac health. It, also, can be instrumental in lowering "bad" (LDL) cholesterol levels while raising the "good" (HDL) ones.

Dining Out

Dining out is easy – just don't forget your carb counter! Be careful of the bread, crackers, rice, pasta, potatoes and dessert unless you've saved enough carb grams for the day to splurge.

For luncheon items, stick with protein and salads without the croutons. Creative, low carb selections can be the ingredients of a ham sandwich between two pieces of cheese instead of bread, a cheeseburger "all the way" but without the bun or just the topping of your favorite pizza. Other lunch choices can include tuna salad atop sliced tomatoes, a grilled chicken Caesar salad or an avocado stuffed with shrimp. Even if dining at a fast food restaurant, omit the bun, fries, cola and enjoy most everything else.

Dining out at dinnertime, also, offers many choices. For example, you may begin with a shrimp remoulade, buffalo wings or paté. Salads are great with most dressings; you will find that Blue cheese is, usually, the lowest in carbs. Choose any meats, poultry or seafood, baked, broiled, grilled or roasted that can be served with any flourless sauce. Vegetables, too, can be safely topped with butter or hollandaise sauce. After dinner, strawberries with whipped cream and assorted cheeses are always winners.

Snacks

Why do we believe in snacks? ... For the simple reason that a healthy snack or two within your daily carb allotment, actually, can be good for you. Of course, when we say "snacks," we do not mean junk food. Healthy snacking should keep your blood sugar from dropping, too low and your metabolism from slowing down. Snacks can be creative, delicious and gratifying, too. The following list should satisfy your craving:

Beef jerky

Cheeses, assorted

Cheese spreads with low carb cracker or raw vegetable

Chicken salad

Cottage cheese

Dill pickles

Dips and tapenades with low carb cracker or raw vegetable

Eggs, deviled or hard-boiled

Egg salad

Fruit

Guacamole with low carb cracker or raw vegetable

Jell-O sugar free gelatin snacks

Meat, poultry or seafood with condiments

Nuts, assorted

Olives, black, green, Kalamata or stuffed

Peanut butter, all natural and unsweetened

Pickled or marinated vegetables

Pork rinds

Preserves, natural whole fruit with no sugar added

Sardines and sliced onions

Smoked clams and oysters

Smoothie, sugar free

Tofu

Tuna salad

Yogurt, frozen and sugar free

Yogurt, natural and sugar free

Personal Pointers

Now, we will share with you various tips for success from firsthand experience. Hopefully, some tips, if not all, will prove instrumental for you in maintaining a low carb lifestyle as they have for us. Certainly, determination, commitment and discipline are most significant in fulfilling weight loss goals. On the other hand, strict adherence all of the time to the rules of the diet game can be unrealistic and is not always necessary. In other words, sometimes, just a tad bit of cheating will help you win. The following list of winning tricks should help you lose weight and stay on track while you *PLAY YOUR CARBS RIGHT!... WITH THE BRENNANS*:

- Advance preparation of healthy, low carb ingredients for meals and snacks will prevent the temptation to eat the wrong foods that are readily available.

- Never allow yourself to become very hungry. You are likely to eat anything in sight – healthy or not. This is another reason to have ingredients for low carb meals and snacks already prepared.

- Do not eat if you are not hungry; and never feel compelled to eat everything on your plate, despite the fact your mother told you to do so.

- At breakfast time, be open-minded. Except for eggs, bacon, ham and sausage, other traditional breakfast foods, such as bagels, cereals, donuts, French toast, grits, oatmeal, pancakes and waffles, are extremely high in carbs. Oftentimes, our favorite low carb substitutes are leftovers. A broiled chicken breast, a slice of pot roast or the broccoli au gratin from the night before may sound crazy but are satisfying and delicious. Tuna, chicken and other salads are additional options to consider.

- For the person "on the go," food choices at lunchtime are not always good choices. In particular, fast food can be too easily available as can other equally bad choices. Therefore, advance consideration and preparation of lunch is most helpful for achieving set goals and avoiding such pitfalls.

- Luncheon tricks include eating only half of the hamburger bun or one slice of sandwich bread. Sandwiches with lettuce, tomato, mustard and mayonnaise may be prepared between two slices of cheese; and burritos, tacos and other fillings may be rolled with a large lettuce leaf instead of the traditional shell.

- Dinner, as we know it, may be eaten midday instead. Some people prefer luncheon items as a light evening fare and benefit from reversing luncheon and dinner choices.

- Out to lunch or dinner and forgot your carb counter? You can always play it safe by sticking with protein and a green salad or vegetable. If you are served a pre-ordered meal, just eat the meat, chicken or seafood and whatever green accompanies the main dish.

- Drinking too much of any beverage during the course of a meal interferes with digestion.

- It is never wise to eat right before going to bed as, most definitely, you will pack on extra pounds. A late night meal can cause indigestion, and most cholesterol is produced at night.

- Cravings can destroy the best intentions and the strongest commitment for weight loss – so eat it! Get whatever it is out of your system. You don't have to eat the whole thing; sometimes a bite or two will do. You may surprise yourself and discover that whatever craving you ate may have fit into your daily carb allowance. Whether it did or not, just do it; get it over with and then move on! Your diet will not be ruined, and you will feel satisfied and rewarded.

- We, also, are firm believers in occasional splurges as realistic means to maintain a long term, low carb lifestyle. In other words, your choices of carbs do not always have to be the most, healthy ones as long as you do not exceed your daily carb limit. For example, a half of a loaded baked potato or a small dish of ice cream is O.K. We even have a friend who was successful eating salads during the day and a few miniature candy bars for dinner. Sometimes, whether dining out or at home, it is necessary to save your daily carb allotment for a special meal or for an important occasion. Just remember, that we are only advocating occasional splurges and that a steady diet of high carbohydrate foods is unhealthy and can cause disease.

- Don't drive yourself crazy weighing yourself twice a day. We do not even recommend weighing yourself twice a week – once a week or less is plenty. First thing in the morning is the best time of day to determine weight loss success.

Maintenance

Once your desired weight is realized, you may, gradually, increase your daily carbohydrate intake. We suggest that you slowly increase your daily intake by 5 to 7 grams one week at a time. In other words, if you have been maintaining a daily intake of 40 grams per day, then we recommend for one week that you maintain 45 to 47 grams of carbohydrates per day.

At the end of the first week, if you are still losing weight, then you may repeat this process one week at a time until your weight loss has stopped, and your desired weight stabilizes. Just be very careful to monitor yourself closely! You do not want to gain any significant weight in this process. When you do reach a daily carb count that triggers weight gain then, merely, return to the previous week's daily carb allowance.

In other words, you are trying to determine the maximum carb grams you can consume daily without gaining weight. An average daily consumption for maintenance can reach and even exceed 75 grams of carbohydrates a day; sometimes, maintenance levels need to be less. You must scrutinize your daily carb intake and determine the maintenance formula for you.

Determining precisely your maintenance level needs to be a gradual process. However, as the process progresses and additional carb grams are allowed daily, we recommend that you choose healthy carbohydrates, such as beans, additional fruit, sweet potatoes, yams, whole grains (such as brown rice, oatmeal, wild rice) and whole grain breads, cereals and pasta. These particular carbs, most probably, have not been included in your diet until now as their gram count can be high for weight loss, but their nutritional value, rich in vitamins and fiber, cannot be ignored.

You may include many of these healthy carbs with our recipes. Brown or wild rice, sweet potatoes or whole grain pasta make delicious, healthy and satisfying side dishes. The words "whole grain" are key, not enriched or refined; of course, always be cautious of processing and packaging. As we have already explained, read the labels and avoid any unhealthy, unacceptable ingredients.

14 Daily Menus

The following daily menus will help you maintain your low carb lifestyle with very little guesswork. The carb count for each day is deliberately low. This will allow you to supplement each day with snacks or additional food items of your choice. Remember that these are only suggested menus. Feel free to delete anything. Substitution at any meal of a different recipe or one of your own creation is acceptable as long as you do not exceed your daily carb gram allowance.

As we explained in "Personal Pointers," be open-minded at breakfast and do not hesitate to begin the day with leftovers or other food choices high in protein. Feasting on protein, also, makes gram counting easy. Reference to your gram counter is unnecessary as meat, chicken and fish are gramless. Luncheon and dinner items are interchangeable; therefore, changing the order or eliminating an item altogether is acceptable. Such versatility and creativity will help you implement your new and healthy way of life as you *PLAY YOUR CARBS RIGHT!... WITH THE BRENNANS*.

Week 1

MONDAY	BREAKFAST	LUNCH	DINNER
	1 cup cantaloupe 12.2 grams 1 scrambled egg 0.1 gram 1 strip crisp bacon 0.1 gram	³/₄ cup Tuna Salad* 0.8 gram ¹/₂ cup sliced tomato 4.2 grams	2 Baja Chicken Wraps* 10.6 grams ³/₄ cup Green Bean and Onion Szechwan* 6.6 grams
Daily Total 34.6 grams	Total 12.4 grams	Total 5.0 grams	Total 17.2 grams
TUESDAY	**BREAKFAST**	**LUNCH**	**DINNER**
	1 cup fresh strawberries 2.1 grams 6 oz. light sugar free yogurt 14.0 grams	6-8 oz. hamburger patty-0 grams 1 slice melted cheddar cheese 1.0 gram ¹/₄ cup sliced tomato 2.1 grams 2 tablespoons Blue Cheese and Green Onion Vinaigrette* 1.7 grams	1¹/₂ cups Veal Stew with Artichokes and Mushrooms* 9.0 grams 2 cups chopped iceberg lettuce 3.4 grams 4 tablespoons French Dressing* 1.2 grams
Daily Total 34.5 grams	Total 16.1 grams	Total 4.8 grams	Total 13.6 grams
WEDNESDAY	**BREAKFAST**	**LUNCH**	**DINNER**
	1 slice stone ground whole wheat toast 8.0 grams 1 fried egg 0.1 gram	2 cups Wild, Wild West Salad* 14.35 grams	2 cups Barbecued Shrimp* 6.3 grams 1 cup Tomato and Bacon Spaghetti Squash* 6.0 grams
Daily Total 34.8 grams	Total 8.1 grams	Total 14.35 grams	Total 12.3 grams
THURSDAY	**BREAKFAST**	**LUNCH**	**DINNER**
	1 slice rye toast 14.0 grams ¹/₄ cup Smoked Salmon and Cream Cheese Spread* 1.2 grams	1¹/₄ cups Bangkok Chicken Salad* 9.2 grams	Southern Baked Halibut* 3.6 grams 1 cup Asparagus and Hearts of Palm Vinaigrette* 6.2 grams Broccoli Parmesan* 2.5 grams
Daily Total 36.7 grams	Total 15.2 grams	Total 9.2 grams	Total 12.3 grams

Refer to Index for recipe page number.

Week 1

FRIDAY	BREAKFAST	LUNCH	DINNER
	½ cup fresh blackberries 9.4 grams ½ cup cream 4.0 grams 1 scrambled egg 0.1 gram 2 sugarless sausage links 1.0 gram	2 cups Caesar Salad with Shrimp* 4.0 grams	1 cup Steak Fajita* 10.9 grams 1 cup Mexican Cauliflower* 4.4 grams
Daily Total 33.8 grams	Total 14.5 grams	Total 4.0 grams	Total 15.3 grams

SATURDAY	BREAKFAST	LUNCH	DINNER
	Chicken and Asparagus Frittata* 3.2 grams	1 cup Very Berry Salad* 14.5 grams 2 Tomato Pizzas* 3.1 grams	1 cup Crabmeat Imperial* 6.2 grams 2 cups chopped romaine lettuce 3.2 grams 4 tablespoons Créole Vinaigrette* 2.0 grams Mocha Pudding* 4.6 grams
Daily Total 36.8 grams	Total 3.2 grams	Total 17.6 grams	Total 16.0 grams

SUNDAY	BREAKFAST	LUNCH	DINNER
	1 large slice crustless Quiche Lorraine* 4.2 grams	1½ cups Shrimp Salad* 4.0 grams	¾ cup Pork Marsala* 10.6 grams 1 cup Spicy Eggplant Casserole* 13.8 grams
Daily Total 32.6 grams	Total 4.2 grams	Total 4.0 grams	Total 24.4 grams

Refer to Index for recipe page number.

Week 2

MONDAY	BREAKFAST	LUNCH	DINNER
Daily Total 31.5 grams	1 slice stone ground whole wheat toast 8.0 grams 1 slice melted Swiss cheese 1.0 gram	1 cup Homemade Chicken Salad* 2.9 grams 1 cup chopped iceberg lettuce 1.7 grams	1½ cups Beef Chili* 15.8 grams 1 cup Mixed Green Garlic Salad* 2.1 grams
	Total 9.0 grams	Total 4.6 grams	Total 17.9 grams

TUESDAY	BREAKFAST	LUNCH	DINNER
Daily Total 33.8 grams	Broccoli and Gruyère Cheese Frittata* 3.1 grams	2 cups Italian Salad* 10.0 grams	2 cups Sweet Pepper and Mushroom Chicken* 11.3 grams ³/₄ cup Spinach Walnut Salad* 9.4 grams
	Total 3.1 grams	Total 10.0 grams	Total 20.7 grams

WEDNESDAY	BREAKFAST	LUNCH	DINNER
Daily Total 35.8 grams	1 cup fresh strawberries 2.1 grams ½ cup cream 4.0 grams	1¼ cups Spicy Beef-Broccoli Salad* 9.9 grams	1½ cups Singing Shrimp* 10.3 grams 1½ cups Stewed Okra Evangeline* 9.5 grams
	Total 6.1 grams	Total 9.9 grams	Total 19.8 grams

THURSDAY	BREAKFAST	LUNCH	DINNER
Daily Total 30.6 grams	Tex-Mex Omelette* 8.1 grams	1½ cups Califlower, Cucumber and Tomato Salad* 9.9 grams grilled chicken breast 0 grams	1 cup Swiss-Broccoli Soup* 8.3 grams Dijon Marinated Beef* 0 grams 1 cup Sautéed Zucchini* 4.3 grams
	Total 8.1 grams	Total 9.9 grams	Total 12.6 grams

Refer to Index for recipe page number.

Week 2

FRIDAY	BREAKFAST	LUNCH	DINNER
	1 fried egg 　0.1 gram 1 slice stone ground 　whole wheat 　toast 　8.0 grams	2 cups Seafood 　Salad* 　9.9 grams	Chicken Parmigiana* 　5.5 grams 1 cup Green Beans 　Italian Style* 　6.5 grams 1 cup chopped iceburg 　lettuce - 1.7 grams 2 tablespoons Italian 　Dressing* - 0.9 gram
Daily Total 32.6 grams	Total 8.1 grams	Total 9.9 grams	Total 14.6 grams
SATURDAY	BREAKFAST	LUNCH	DINNER
	1 cup fresh 　strawberries 　2.1 grams 6 oz. light sugar free 　yogurt 　14.0 grams	6-8 oz. hamburger 　patty-0 grams 1 slice melted 　Cheddar cheese 　1.0 gram 1 cup chopped 　romaine lettuce 　1.6 grams 2 tablespoons Ranch 　Dressing* 　1.2 grams	Citrus Salmon with 　Caper Butter* 　1.7 grams Shanghai Spinach* 　2.3 grams 1 cup Avocado, 　Broccoli and 　Pecan Vinaigrette* 　6.7 grams Baked Vanilla 　Custard* 　5. 6 grams
Daily Total 36.2 grams	Total 16.1 grams	Total 3.8 grams	Total 16.3 grams
SUNDAY	BREAKFAST	LUNCH	DINNER
	$1/2$ cup cantaloupe 　6.1 grams Crustless Crabmeat 　Quiche* 　4.3 grams	Buffalo Wings with 　Blue Cheese* 　1.9 grams 1 cup chopped 　iceburg lettuce 　1.7 grams 2 tablespoons 　Classical 　Vinaigrette* 　0.4 gram	Filet Royale* 　1.0 gram 1 cup Asparagus and 　Broccoli Au 　Gratin* 　7.2 grams $1^1/4$ cups Greek 　Tomato Salad* 　9.6 grams
Daily Total 32.2 grams	Total 10.4 grams	Total 4.0 grams	Total 17.8 grams

Refer to Index for recipe page number.

Winning Recipes

Our recipe section is a perfect blend of easy, low carb dishes. Most diets, whether for weight loss or for maintaining good health, seem to limit variety and flavor in the foods permissible when dining. As we tout delicious, healthy and satisfying meals, our recipes prevent any inevitable boredom.

PLAY YOUR CARBS RIGHT!... WITH THE BRENNANS exemplifies the flexibility prevalent in a low carb lifestyle - one that can be realistically maintained forever. You can now say "good-bye" to the monotony of unimaginative menus as our selection of recipes will create enthusiasm for maintaining a low carb way of life.

Certain ingredients should be prepared in advance to facilitate many recipes. For example, mayonnaise, salad dressings and ice cream may be prepared ahead of time to expedite meals. This extra prep time will simplify and alleviate the hassle of a hurried dinner hour. We might add that such advance preparation will, also, avoid the temptation to use ingredients readily available that are high in carbs.

In our recipes, you may choose to modify your fat intake whenever possible. Remember to use lean cuts of meat and skinless chicken in order to reduce saturated fat intake. Instead of butter, certainly, canola and olive oils are two of your best choices. You may substitute skim, low fat or even whole milk for cream. Just remember that many times low fat and no fat can equate to high carbohydrate content. If a recipe calls for cream or whole milk, a "tip" worth trying is to dilute a lesser amount of cream with water; but know that low fat modifications will alter the consistency of soups and sauces making them thin in texture.

When any of our recipes required an artificial sweetener, we chose Sweet 'N

Low.® However, for health reasons, it is important to know that most artificial sweeteners should be used with caution and in moderation. Alternating the use of various conventional sweeteners will reduce the ingestion of significant amounts of any one kind – thus diminishing the risk of potential side effects.

Furthermore, whenever possible, we highly recommend the use of two natural sugar substitutes – the all natural Ki-Sweet® and the naturally, sweet herb Stevia®. It is believed that both of these natural sweeteners do not have the adverse side effects of many commonly used artificial sweeteners.

Significantly, most natural sugar substitutes as well as conventional artificial sweeteners, such as aspartame, saccharin, acesulfame-k and sucralose as well as the sugar alcohols isomalt, maltitol, mannitol, sorbitol and xylitol, are carbohydrates. Remember that because they are all carbohydrates, their gram content, even if only fractional, adds up, and, therefore, must be counted.

Our recipes should make losing weight quick, simple and healthy. We have fascilitated carb counting with a break down of carbohydrates per serving, referred to as "carb grams" in each recipe. You will enjoy our collection of both creative and traditional dishes – all great tasting, satisfying and from your very own kitchen. Enjoy feasting on luscious food while knowing that overall good health and delicious dining are yours when you *PLAY YOUR CARBS RIGHT!... WITH THE BRENNANS.*

Appetizers

Stilton, Celery and Chive Spread

1 cup Stilton cheese, room temperature

1 cup cream cheese, room temperature

6 tablespoons celery, finely chopped

6 tablespoons chopped chives

Dash Tabasco®

Serves eight – 1.5 carb grams per serving

Combine all ingredients thoroughly in a medium-sized bowl. Chill and serve with celery sticks or another low carb vegetable for dipping.

Green Olive Spread

$^1/_2$ cup unsalted butter or margarine

2 medium onions, finely chopped

2 tablespoons chopped red pepper

16 oz. cream cheese, room temperature

16 oz. green olives, pitted, drained and finely chopped

1 teaspoon chili powder

Serves twelve – 4 carb grams per serving

Melt butter or margarine in small saucepan, add onions, peppers and sauté until soft; allow to cool. Thoroughly blend cream cheese with butter/onion/pepper mixture in a medium-sized bowl. Then fold in the olives and chili powder. Place in a serving bowl; chill and serve with any low carb vegetable for dipping.

Black Olive Tapenade

4 oz. anchovy fillets

$1\frac{1}{2}$ cups black olives, pitted, drained and finely chopped

$\frac{1}{2}$ cup capers, finely chopped

$\frac{1}{2}$ cup olive oil

2 teaspoons garlic, minced

2 teaspoons black pepper

Serves six – 3.4 carb grams per serving

Rinse and drain anchovy fillets. Mix in a medium-sized bowl with the remaining ingredients. Blend in a food processor until the mixture attains a coarse consistency. Place in a serving bowl; chill and serve with any low carb vegetable for dipping.

Baked Crabmeat Spread

2 cups crabmeat

1 cup grated sharp Cheddar cheese

$\frac{1}{2}$ cup green onion, finely chopped

$\frac{1}{4}$ cup green pepper, finely chopped

$\frac{1}{2}$ cup mayonnaise

4 Dashes Tabasco®

2 Dashes Worcestershire sauce

salt and pepper to taste

Preheat oven to 450° F.

Serves eight – 1.4 carb grams per serving

In a bowl, combine all the ingredients and mix gently. Place mixture in a well greased 9 inch square pan. Bake in oven for 6 to 8 minutes or until cheese has visibly melted.

Cold Crabmeat with Pepper Sauce

3 cups crabmeat

1¹/₂ cups chopped green onion

¹/₂ cup parsley, finely chopped

1 tablespoon lemon juice

3 Dashes Worcestershire sauce

1 tablespoon Tabasco®

2 tablespoons water

2 cups mayonnaise

salt and pepper to taste

Serves six – 3.7 carb grams per serving

Except for the crabmeat, combine all other ingredients in a food processor and blend until smooth; then chill. Divide the crabmeat among six individual plates and top with pepper sauce. Serve and enjoy!

Smoked Salmon and Cream Cheese Spread

16 oz. cream cheese, room temperature

1 cup chopped smoked salmon

2 tablespoons mayonnaise

¹/₂ teaspoon lemon juice

¹/₂ teaspoon garlic powder

1 teaspoon Worcestershire sauce

¹/₂ teaspoon Tabasco®

Serves six – 2.4 carb grams per serving

Mix all ingredients together and chill. May be served with any low carb vegetable.

Salmon Tartare with Cucumber Slices

2 cups chopped smoked salmon

$^1/_2$ cup onion, finely chopped

1 teaspoon salt

$^1/_2$ teaspoon black pepper

$^1/_4$ cup olive oil

1 teaspoon Tabasco®

1 teaspoon fresh lemon juice

3 tablespoons fresh chopped chives

1 tablespoon fresh chopped basil

2 large cucumbers, peeled and sliced

Serves eight – 2.8 carb grams per serving

Mix all ingredients together and chill. Serve atop individual cucumber slices.

Fresh Guacamole

4 ripe avocados, peeled and pitted

2 plum tomatoes, peeled and chopped

1 medium onion, finely chopped

4 chopped chile peppers

2 tablespoons lime juice

1 teaspoon garlic, minced

1 tablespoon fresh cilantro, minced

1 teaspoon Tabasco®

salt and pepper to taste

Serves eight – 11.9 carb grams per serving

Except for the tomatoes, onion and chile peppers, blend all other ingredients in a food processor until smooth. Pour mixture into a bowl and gently mix in tomatoes, onion and chile peppers by hand. Place avocado seed in the bowl to prevent darkening of guacamole. Chill in a covered container; then serve.

South of the Border Salsa

6 medium tomatoes, finely chopped

1 small onion, finely chopped

$^1/_2$ teaspoon salt

2 tablespoons fresh lime juice

2 tablespoons fresh cilantro, finely chopped

1 jalapeno pepper, minced

2 tablespoons fresh parsley, finely chopped

1 teaspoon garlic, minced

1 cup olive oil

5 Dashes Tabasco®

Serves eight – 6.3 carb grams per serving

Combine all ingredients in a bowl and mix well. Cover and chill for at least 3 hours; then serve.

Fresh Garden Herb Dip

$1^1/_2$ cups cream cheese, room temperature

1 cup sour cream

1 large cucumber, peeled and chopped

$^1/_2$ cup green onion, finely chopped

2 teaspoons garlic, minced

2 tablespoons fresh parsley, finely chopped

1 tablespoon fresh tarragon, finely chopped

3 teaspoons capers, finely chopped

1 teaspoon fresh lemon juice

3 tablespoons olive oil

$^1/_4$ teaspoon cayenne pepper

$^1/_2$ teaspoon salt

Serves six – 5.7 carb grams per serving

Combine all ingredients in a food processor until smooth. Place the mixture in a serving bowl; cover and refrigerate for at least 2 hours. May be served with any low carb vegetable for dipping.

Alaña's Spiñach and Artichoke Dip

10 oz. artichoke hearts, drained and chopped

10 oz. frozen chopped spinach, thawed and drained

1 teaspoon salt

$^1/_2$ teaspoon black pepper

$^1/_2$ teaspoon celery salt

$^1/_4$ teaspoon nutmeg

$^3/_2$ teaspoon garlic powder

$^1/_2$ teaspoon Tabasco®

$1^1/_2$ cups cream cheese, room temperature

2 tablespoons plus 1 cup mayonnaise

$^3/_4$ cup parsley, finely chopped

$^3/_4$ cup onion, finely chopped

1 teaspoon lemon juice

2 cups shredded Mozzarella cheese

Preheat oven to 350° F.

Serves ten – 6.54 carb grams per serving

Sauté spinach and the 2 tablespoons of mayonnaise together over medium-high heat until spinach turns dark green. In a bowl, mix the spinach with all remaining ingredients, except Mozzarella cheese. Place the mixture in a baking dish and cover with all of the Mozzarella cheese. Bake for 15 to 20 minutes, or until cheese is bubbling and golden. May serve atop Parmesan Crackers (recipe immediately follows).

Parmesan Crackers

$^1/_2$ lb. freshly grated Parmesan cheese

Serves four – 2.1 carb grams per serving

Place a non-stick skillet over medium heat. Drop tablespoons of the Parmesan cheese into the skillet. Flatten each spoonful of cheese into cracker size. Cook the wafers on each side for about 3 minutes, until crisp or golden brown. Transfer crackers to a plate and allow to cool before serving.

Blue Cheese Paté

8 oz. Blue cheese, room temperature

6 oz. cream cheese, room temperature

4 tablespoons lemon juice

2 tablespoons chopped chives

1 teaspoon paprika

Serves eight – 2.1 carb grams per serving

Blend the Blue cheese, lemon juice and cream cheese together in a bowl or food processor. Thoroughly mix in chives and paprika by hand. Chill and serve with any low carb vegetable for dipping.

Chicken Liver Paté

$^1/_2$ cup cooking oil

2 cups butter or margarine

2 lbs. chicken livers

2 medium onions, quartered

4 hard-boiled eggs, peeled and coarsely chopped

$^1/_2$ teaspoon salt

Serves eight – 7.7 carb grams per serving

Heat cooking oil in large saucepan. Add chicken livers; cover and simmer over low heat for 10-15 minutes. Strain chicken livers in a colander and purée in a food processor. Transfer the puréed chicken livers to a medium-sized bowl. Purée onion in the food processor, then transfer to the same bowl. Purée hard-boiled eggs in the food processor, then thoroughly mix them with the chicken livers and onion. Melt the butter or margarine and add to the mixture with salt.

Return the chicken liver mixture to the food processor until a smooth consistency is attained. Additional salt may be added to taste. Chicken liver paté may be served either warm or chilled.

Cheese Ball Amandine

8 oz. sharp Cheddar cheese, room temperature

8 oz. cream cheese, room temperature

3 oz. Stilton cheese, room temperature

1 teaspoon garlic, minced

1 tablespoon Worcestershire sauce

$^3/_4$ cup almonds, finely chopped

$^1/_2$ cup fresh parsley, finely chopped

$^1/_4$ teaspoon Tabasco®

Serves six – 6.1 carb grams per serving

Break the cheese into pieces and place in a food processor. Add the garlic, Worcestershire sauce, Tabasco® and blend until creamy. Pour the mixture into a medium-sized bowl and stir in $^1/_2$ cup of the almonds; chill until firm enough to shape into a ball.

Roll the cheese ball into a mixture of the parsley and remaining $^1/_4$ cup of almonds until covered. Refrigerate for 24 hours before serving. May be served with any low carb vegetable for dipping.

Tomato Pizzas

8 slices tomato

8 slices Mozzarella cheese

1 teaspoon dried basil

8 thin slices pepperoni

4 tablespoons olive oil

4 tablespoons freshly grated Parmesan cheese

Preheat oven to 425° F.

Serves four – 3.1 carb grams per serving

On each slice of tomato, place a slice of Mozzarella cheese; sprinkle with basil. Cover each portion with a slice of pepperoni; then drizzle all eight tomato pizzas with olive oil and sprinkle with Parmesan cheese. Bake in oven for 6 to 10 minutes or until cheese has melted. Serve and enjoy!

Pitty Pat Deviled Eggs

6 large eggs, hard-boiled and peeled

2 teaspoons yellow mustard

3 tablespoons mayonnaise

$^1/_4$ teaspoon salt

$^1/_2$ teaspoon black pepper

Paprika for garnish

Serves six – 0.9 carb grams per serving

After the eggs have cooled, halve the eggs lengthwise and carefully scoop out the yolks. In a bowl, mash the yolks with a fork; then add the mustard, mayonnaise, salt and pepper, blending well. Fill the whites with the egg yolk mixture and sprinkle the tops with paprika.

Smoked Salmon Stuffed Eggs

6 large eggs, hard-boiled and peeled

$^1/_3$ cup smoked salmon, finely chopped

$^1/_4$ cup onion, finely chopped

$^1/_3$ cup capers, finely chopped

$^1/_4$ teaspoon salt

$^1/_4$ teaspoon black pepper

$^1/_2$ cup mayonnaise

2 tablespoons fresh parsley, finely chopped

Serves six – 1.8 carb grams per serving

After the eggs have cooled, halve the eggs lengthwise and carefully scoop out the yolks. In a bowl, mash the yolks with a fork; then add salmon, onion, capers, salt, pepper and mayonnaise, blending well. Fill the whites with the egg yolk mixture and sprinkle the tops with parsley.

Stuffed Eggs Calcutta

6 large eggs, hard-boiled and peeled

2 teaspoons curry powder

1 1/2 teaspoons soy sauce

1/4 teaspoon salt

1/4 teaspoon black pepper

1/2 cup mayonnaise

2 tablespoons fresh parsley, finely chopped

Serves six – 1.4 carb grams per serving

After the eggs have cooled, halve the eggs lengthwise and carefully scoop out the yolks. In a bowl, mash the yolks with a fork; then add curry powder, soy sauce, salt, pepper and mayonnaise, blending well. Fill the whites with the egg yolk mixture and sprinkle the tops with parsley.

Mushrooms Florentine

24 large fresh mushrooms

20 oz. frozen chopped spinach

6 oz. cream cheese, room temperature

1 cup green onion, finely chopped

1/2 teaspoon salt

1/2 teaspoon black pepper

1/8 teaspoon nutmeg

1/2 cup olive oil

Serves twelve – 4.9 carb grams per serving

Wash the mushrooms and remove the stems; then on a cooking sheet, place each mushroom bottom side up. Following the package directions, cook the spinach; then drain thoroughly. In a medium-sized bowl, blend the spinach, cream cheese, onion, salt, pepper and nutmeg. Place a spoonful of the spinach mixture atop each mushroom. Heat the olive oil and fry the mushroom bottoms until lightly browned. Serve immediately.

Mushrooms Vinaigrette

²/₃ cup balsamic vinegar

²/₃ cup dry white wine

2 teaspoons dried oregano

1 small red pepper, sliced

1 dried hot chile pepper, crumbled

4 whole cloves garlic

2 tablespoons fresh parsley, finely chopped

1 lemon, seeded and cut into quarters

1 lb. fresh mushrooms

3 tablespoons olive oil

Serves four – 4.6 carb grams per serving

Trim off the stems of the mushrooms; then wash well and pat dry with paper towel. Except for the mushrooms and olive oil, combine all other ingredients in a large saucepan and bring to a boil; then add the mushrooms. Sprinkle mixture with the olive oil and boil for 6 to 7 minutes. Turn off the heat, allowing the mushrooms to cool before serving with toothpicks.

Classic Buffalo Wings

10 lbs. chicken wings

1 cup butter or margarine

1¹/₂ cups hot pepper sauce

Celery sticks

2 cups Blue cheese dressing (see Index)

Preheat oven to 425° F.

Serves eight – 0.4 carb grams per serving without Blue Cheese Dressing

1.9 carb grams per serving with Blue Cheese Dressing

Split the chicken wings at each joint and discard the tips; rinse, then pat dry. On baking sheets, place the wings and bake for 30 minutes. Turn and bake the chicken wings for an additional 30 minutes or until golden brown. Drain the chicken well; then place in a large bowl.

In a saucepan, melt the butter or margarine over medium-low heat and stir in the hot pepper sauce. Pour over the cooked chicken wings and mix well until thoroughly coated. Serve immediately with Blue cheese dressing and celery sticks.

Chinese Meatballs

1 lb. lean ground meat

1 lb. lean ground pork

2 eggs, beaten

1 cup chopped water chestnuts

2 tablespoons fresh ginger, finely chopped

1 teaspoon garlic, minced

2 tablespoons sesame oil

2 tablespoons soy sauce

1 teaspoon salt

1 teaspoon black pepper

4 tablespoons cooking oil for frying

Serves twenty – 1.3 carb grams per serving

Except for the cooking oil, combine all other ingredients in a bowl. Form the meat mixture into individual round balls, about 1-2 inches in diameter. Heat the cooking oil and fry the meatballs on all sides until done. Serve with toothpicks and enjoy!

Spicy Beef Rolls

8 oz. cream cheese, room temperature

3 tablespoons horseradish

3 tablespoons chives, finely chopped

$^1/_3$ cup sour cream

$^1/_4$ teaspoon salt

2 Dashes Tabasco®

6 thin slices roast beef

Serves six – 2.6 carb grams per serving

Except for the roast beef, blend all other ingredients in a food processor. Lay roast beef slices on a platter and spread each slice with a layer of the mixture. Roll up each slice individually and secure with a toothpick. For additional servings, may be cut into smaller portions.

Roquefort Chicken Rolls

8 oz. Roquefort cheese, room temperature

8 oz. cream cheese, room temperature

$^1/_3$ cup sour cream

$^1/_2$ teaspoon garlic, minced

$^1/_4$ teaspoon salt

$^1/_4$ teaspoon black pepper

8 thin slices chicken breasts

Serves eight – 2.1 carb grams per serving

Except for the slices of chicken breasts, blend all other ingredients in a food processor. Lay chicken slices on a platter and spread each slice with a layer of the mixture. Roll up each slice individually and secure with a toothpick. For additional servings, may be cut into smaller portions.

Sauces

Hollandaise Sauce

2 cups butter or margarine

4 egg yolks

1^1/$_2$ teaspoons red wine vinegar

1 teaspoon salt

pinch of cayenne pepper

1^1/$_2$ teaspoons water

Yields 2 cups – 0.1 carb grams per 2 Tablespoons

In a medium saucepan, melt the butter or margarine; skim and discard the milk solids from the top of the butter or margarine. Hold the clarified butter or margarine over very low heat while preparing the eggs yolks.

Place the egg yolks, vinegar, salt and cayenne pepper in a large bowl and whisk briefly. Fill a saucepan, large enough to accommodate the bowl, with about 1 inch of water. Heat the water to just below the boiling point and set the bowl in the saucepan.

Whisk the egg yolk mixture until slightly thickened, then drizzle the butter or margarine into the yolks, whisking constantly. When all of the butter or margarine is incorporated and the sauce is thick, beat in the water.

Serve the Hollandaise sauce immediately or keep in a warm place at room temperature until use.

Béarnaise Sauce

2 cups butter or margarine
4 egg yolks
1^1/$_2$ teaspoons red wine vinegar
1 teaspoon salt
pinch of cayenne pepper
1^1/$_2$ teaspoons water
1 tablespoon tarragon vinegar
1 tablespoon dry white wine
1 tablespoon green onion, finely chopped
1 tablespoon capers, drained
1 tablespoon parsley, finely chopped

Yields 2 cups – 0.2 carb grams per 2 Tablespoons

In a medium saucepan, melt the butter or margarine; skim and discard the milk solids from the top of the butter or margarine. Hold the clarified butter or margarine over very low heat while preparing the eggs yolks.

Place the egg yolks, vinegar, salt and cayenne pepper in a large bowl and whisk briefly. Fill a saucepan, large enough to accommodate the bowl, with about 1 inch of water. Heat the water to just below the boiling point and set the bowl in the saucepan.

Whisk the egg yolk mixture until slightly thickened, then drizzle the butter or margarine into the yolks, whisking constantly. When all of the butter or margarine is incorporated and the sauce is thick, beat in the water. Fold in the vinegar, wine, green onion, capers and parsley.

Serve the Béarnaise sauce immediately or keep in a warm place at room temperature until use.

Garlic Butter Sauce

1 cup butter or margarine, room temperature

2 teaspoons Worcestershire sauce

6 garlic cloves, minced

2 teaspoons parsley, finely chopped

2 teaspoons Tabasco®

pinch of salt

Yields 1 cup – 1.0 carb gram per 2 Tablespoons

Combine all ingredients in a small bowl and blend thoroughly. Should be warm when used atop main dishes and vegetables.

Lemon Butter Sauce

4 cups butter or margarine

juice of 4 lemons

$^1/_4$ cup white wine vinegar

Yields 4 cups – 0.6 carb gram per 2 Tablespoons

In a medium saucepan, lightly brown butter or margarine. Add lemon juice and vinegar while stirring over a low heat for 10 minutes. Should be warm when used atop main dishes and vegetables.

Pecan Butter Sauce

$^1/_2$ cup chopped pecans

3 tablespoons lemon juice

2 teaspoons Worcestershire sauce

Dash Tabasco®

2 tablespoons green onion, finely chopped

$^1/_2$ cup butter or margarine, melted

$^1/_2$ teaspoon salt

$^1/_4$ teaspoon white pepper

Yields 1 cup – 1.9 carb grams per 2 Tablespoons

In a bowl, combine all ingredients; heat and serve over baked, broiled or grilled fish.

Steak Sauce

8 tablespoons butter or margarine

8 green onions, finely chopped

2 garlic cloves, minced

2 tablespoons Dijon mustard

2 tablespoons dry white wine

2 teaspoons Worcestershire sauce

Yields 1 cup – 1.4 carb grams per 2 Tablespoons

In a small pan, over medium heat, sauté the green onion and garlic in the butter or margarine for about 2 minutes. Stir constantly and slowly add the remaining ingredients; then serve immediately.

Alfredo Sauce

³/4 cup butter or margarine

2 cups grated Parmesan cheese

1 cup cream

1 cup milk

¹/2 cup parsley, finely chopped

freshly ground black pepper to taste

Yields 5 cups – 1.4 carb grams per 2 Tablespoons

In a saucepan, melt the butter or margarine and gently stir in the cheese. Add the cream and milk, heating thoroughly, but carefully not to boil. Stir in the parsley and black pepper; then serve over chicken or veal.

Tomato Sauce

12 cups ripe tomatoes, peeled and chopped

1¹/2 cups chopped onion

4 garlic cloves, minced

¹/4 cup olive oil

2 tablespoons tomato paste

¹/2 cup dry red wine

¹/2 cup chopped basil leaves

¹/2 cup chopped parsley

2 teaspoons oregano

¹/2 teaspoon crushed red pepper

salt and pepper to taste

pinch of granulated Sweet 'N Low®

Yields 8 cups – 8.5 carb grams per ¹/2 cup

In a large pot, heat the oil and sauté the green onion and garlic over medium heat for about 4 minutes. Stir in the tomatoes and the remaining ingredients; simmer until the tomatoes form a sauce for about 30 minutes. Season with the salt and pepper to taste; then mix in the Sweet 'N Low.® May be served atop meat, chicken or veal.

Horseradish Sauce

1 cup sour cream

3 tablespoons horseradish

$^1/_4$ teaspoon salt

$^1/_4$ teaspoon white pepper

$^1/_4$ teaspoon lemon juice

Yields 1 cup – 1.9 carb grams per 2 Tablespoons

In a food processor, thoroughly combine all the ingredients; then serve.

Fresh Mint Sauce

4 tablespoons Dijon mustard

6 tablespoons dry white wine

$1^1/_2$ cups balsamic vinegar

4 tablespoons fresh mint, minced

Yields 2 cups – 5.1 carb grams per 2 Tablespoons

In a food processor, thoroughly combine all of the ingredients before serving with beef or lamb.

57

Ketchup

15 oz. tomato sauce

6 oz. tomato paste

2 tablespoons red wine vinegar

$1^1/_2$ teaspoons onion powder

$1^1/_2$ teaspoons garlic powder

$^1/_4$ teaspoon salt

$^1/_2$ teaspoon Tabasco®

$^1/_2$ teaspoon granulated Sweet 'N Low®

Yields 2$^1/_2$ cups – 3.0 carb grams per 2 Tablespoons

Except for the Sweet 'N Low,® cook all other ingredients in a saucepan over medium-high heat and slowly bring to a boil. Remove from the heat and allow to cool. Once mixture reaches room temperature, stir in the Sweet 'N Low.® Serve immediately or refrigerate.

Tartar Sauce

2 cups mayonnaise

$^1/_2$ cup chopped onion

$^1/_2$ cup chopped dill pickle, drained

1 teaspoon lemon juice

Yields 3 cups – 0.6 carb grams per 2 Tablespoons

In a bowl, thoroughly combine all ingredients by hand. Refrigerate for at least 1 hour before serving.

Soups

The Cheesiest Cheddar Soup

2 cups chopped onion

1 cup chopped celery

$^1/_2$ cup butter or margarine

$^1/_4$ teaspoon cayenne pepper

$^1/_2$ teaspoon dry mustard

3 cups chicken broth or stock

2 cups cream

1 lb. shredded Cheddar cheese

Paprika for garnish

Serves six – 9.1 carb grams per serving

In a saucepan, melt the butter or margarine and sauté the onion and celery until soft. Gradually, stir in the cayenne pepper and dry mustard; cook over low heat until bubbly. Remove the soup from the heat; add the chicken broth or stock and cream. Bring to a boil over medium-high heat, stirring constantly. Reduce to low heat and gradually stir in the cheese; cook only until cheese has melted. Sprinkle each individual serving with paprika for garnish.

Wein's Spicy Chicken Soup

7-8 lb. hen

2 bunches parsley

2 bunches celery

2 large onions

3 teaspoons garlic, minced

5 quarts water

6 dried small red chile peppers

$^1/_2$ teaspoon ginger

salt and pepper to taste

8 scallions, minced for garnish

Serves ten – 4.8 carb grams per serving

In a large pot, place all ingredients, except salt, pepper and scallions. Bring to a boil; lower fire to a slow boil and cook for 2 hours, constantly skimming the residue. Take out hen; strain all vegetables, chop parsley and cut celery into 1 inch pieces. Return parsley and celery to soup; salt and pepper to taste. Serve and garnish with minced scallions.

Anything Goes Swiss-Broccoli Soup

3 cups chicken broth or stock

20 oz. frozen chopped broccoli, thawed and drained

2 cups cream

2 cups milk

$1^1/2$ cups shredded Swiss cheese

salt and pepper to taste

Serves six – 12.5 carb grams per serving

In a 3 quart saucepan, simmer broccoli in chicken broth or stock until tender. Add cream and milk, heating thoroughly; do not boil. Stir in Swiss cheese and cook until cheese has just melted. Serve immediately and enjoy!

Cream of Broccoli Soup

$^1/2$ cup chopped onion

$^1/2$ cup butter or margarine

20 oz. frozen chopped broccoli, thawed and drained

4 cups chicken broth or stock

$^3/4$ teaspoon basil

1 teaspoon salt

$^1/4$ teaspoon black pepper

1 tablespoon lemon juice

1 cup cream

Serves six – 8.4 carb grams per serving

Sauté onion in butter or margarine for about 5 minutes. Add broccoli, chicken broth or stock, basil, salt and pepper. Cover and simmer until broccoli is tender. Pour mixture into a food processor and purée until smooth. Return the soup to a pot and reheat, gradually stirring in the lemon juice and cream. Serve immediately.

A Vegetarian's Vegetable Soup

1/2 cup cooking oil

4 cups fresh mushrooms, sliced

2 cups chopped celery

1 cup chopped onion

1 tablespoon garlic, minced

2 tablespoons fresh parsley, finely chopped

8 cups chicken broth or stock

2 cups chopped broccoli

2 cups chopped cabbage

2 cups chopped tomato

1/2 teaspoon thyme

1/2 teaspoon salt

1/4 teaspoon cayenne pepper

1 cup chopped spinach

3 tablespoons freshly grated Parmesan cheese

Serves eight – 10.4 carb grams per serving

Heat the cooking oil and sauté the mushrooms, celery, onion, garlic and parsley until soft. Add chicken broth or stock, broccoli, cabbage, tomato, thyme, salt and pepper. Cook on low heat for 30 minutes. Add spinach and cheese, cooking for an additional 5 minutes. Enjoy!

Beef and Veggie Soup

8 lb. beef brisket, chuck or rump roast

2 tablespoons salt

2 tablespoons black pepper

4 quarts water

2 lbs. fresh green beans, cut into 1 inch pieces

2 bunches celery, cut into 1 inch pieces

2 large onions, cut into 6 pieces each

2 green peppers, coarsely chopped

2 teaspoons garlic, minced

2 29 oz. cans tomato sauce

2 tablespoons garlic powder

3 tablespoons Worcestershire sauce

1 teaspoon granulated Sweet 'N Low®

1 head cabbage, broken into 2 inch pieces

salt and pepper to taste

Serves sixteen – 18.5 carb grams per serving

Add the meat, salt and pepper to a large pot containing the 4 quarts of water. Boil for 1 hour, skimming the residue from the top of the water as it cooks. Add green beans, celery, onion, green pepper, garlic, garlic powder, tomato sauce, Worcestershire sauce and Sweet 'N Low.® Then add the cabbage and cook for an additional 30 minutes. Add the salt and pepper to taste. Serve meat in soup or on the side with prepared horseradish.

Asparagus Bisque

2 tablespoons olive oil

6 tablespoons butter or margarine

1 cup chopped onion

1 teaspoon garlic, minced

2 lbs. asparagus, peeled and chopped

6 cups chicken broth or stock

$^3/_4$ teaspoon basil

$^1/_2$ teaspoon salt

$^1/_2$ teaspoon black pepper

1 teaspoon Tabasco®

1 tablespoon fresh lemon juice

1 cup cream

Serves six – 11.5 carb gram per serving

In a saucepan, heat the butter or margarine and olive oil; sauté the onion and garlic until soft. Add asparagus and cook for 3 to 4 minutes. Pour in chicken broth or stock, salt, pepper and Tabasco.® Simmer and cook for about 20 minutes until the asparagus are tender. In a food processor, blend the soup until it attains a smooth consistency. Return the soup to the saucepan and stir in the lemon juice and cream to reheat before serving; also may be served chilled.

Cold Avocado Bisque

3 large avocados, peeled and chopped

1 cup chopped tomato

1 cup chopped onion

1 teaspoon garlic, minced

1 cup chopped cucumber

2 cups chicken broth or stock

1 cup cream

1 teaspoon soy sauce

$^1/_4$ teaspoon onion salt

$^1/_2$ teaspoon salt

$^1/_4$ teaspoon white pepper

1 teaspoon fresh lemon juice

3 tablespoons fresh chopped parsley for garnish

Serves eight – 11.2 carb grams per serving

Except for the lemon juice, blend all other ingredients in a food processor until smooth. Cover and chill overnight. Just before serving the cold bisque, stir in the fresh lemon juice and sprinkle each serving with chopped parsley.

Cauliflower and Cheese Soup

20 oz. frozen chopped cauliflower, thawed and drained

10 large fresh mushrooms, sliced

$3^1/_2$ cups chicken broth or stock

1 cup chopped celery

1 cup chopped green onion

1 tablespoon fresh parsley, finely chopped

2 tablespoons butter or margarine

2 teaspoons garlic salt

$^1/_2$ teaspoon Tabasco®

1 teaspoon Worcestershire sauce

$1^1/_2$ cups cream

2 cups grated sharp Cheddar cheese

Serves six – 11.2 carb grams per serving

Cook cauliflower, drain and purée with $1^1/_2$ cups of the chicken broth or stock. In a saucepan, simmer cauliflower with remaining 2 cups chicken broth or stock until tender. In a skillet, melt the butter or margarine and sauté celery, green onion and parsley. Then season the mixture with garlic salt, Tabasco® and Worcestershire sauce. Add cauliflower; cover and cook for 30 minutes. Stir in the cream and blend well. Add the Cheddar cheese and cook until the cheese has just melted; serve immediately.

Curry Spiced Cauliflower Soup

$^3/_4$ cup cooking oil

$1^1/_2$ cups chopped onion

$1^1/_2$ cups chopped celery

2 teaspoons garlic, minced

1 medium-sized jalapeno pepper, minced

2 cups chopped tomato

3 teaspoons curry powder

$1^1/_2$ teaspoons ginger

$1^1/_2$ teaspoons cumin

$1^1/_2$ teaspoons coriander

$1^1/_2$ teaspoons salt

11 cups water

1 large head cauliflower, cut into florets

Serves eight – 11.3 carb grams per serving

Heat the cooking oil in a large saucepan and sauté the onion, celery, garlic and jalapeno pepper until soft. Gradually, stir in the tomatoes and spices, continuing to cook for 2 minutes. Add the water and cauliflower, stirring occasionally. Simmer over medium-low heat for 30 to 40 minutes or until cauliflower is tender. Remove the mixture from the heat and allow to stand for 15 minutes. In a food processor, blend the soup until it attains a smooth consistency. Reheat if necessary, then serve.

Creamy Celery Soup

6 tablespoons butter or margarine

4 cups chopped celery

2 cups milk

4 cups cream

$^1/_8$ teaspoon cayenne pepper

$^1/_2$ teaspoon garlic powder

salt and pepper to taste

Serves six – 11.3 carb grams per serving

Heat the butter or margarine in a large saucepan and sauté the celery until soft. Gradually, mix in the milk and seasonings; bring to a boil, stirring constantly over low heat for about 20 minutes. In a food processor, blend the soup until it attains a smooth consistency. Return the soup to the saucepan and stir in the cream to reheat before serving.

Chilled Cucumber Soup

2 large cucumbers, peeled and chopped

2 cups chopped onion

1 teaspoon garlic, minced

$^1/_2$ teaspoon salt

$^1/_2$ teaspoon white pepper

1 tablespoon Worcestershire sauce

1 teaspoon Tabasco®

2 cups chicken broth or stock

2 cups sour cream

2 tablespoons chopped fresh parsley for garnish

Serves eight – 8.5 carb grams per serving

In a food processor, blend all the ingredients until it attains a smooth consistency. Cover and chill overnight. Sprinkle each individual serving with chopped parsley.

Cream of Mushroom and Onion Soup

1 cup butter or margarine

10 bunches chopped green onion

1 teaspoon garlic, minced

2 teaspoons salt

1 teaspoon white pepper

$^1/_2$ teaspoon cayenne pepper

5 cups chicken broth or stock

5 cups beef broth or stock

2 lbs. mushrooms, thinly sliced

$2^1/_2$ cups cream

Serves ten – 13.2 carb grams per serving

In a saucepan, melt the butter; sauté the green onion, garlic, salt and peppers until soft. Add both broths or stocks and bring to a boil. Cover and simmer for 10 to 15 minutes. In a food processor, blend the soup with 1 lb. of the mushrooms until it attains a smooth consistency. Return the soup to the saucepan and stir in the cream and remaining mushrooms, cooking until tender. Enjoy!

Onion Soup Gratinée

2 tablespoons butter or margarine

1 tablespoon olive oil

2 lbs. onion, thinly sliced

$^1/_8$ teaspoon granulated Sweet 'N Low®

salt and pepper to taste

$^1/_2$ cup dry red wine

6 cups hot beef broth or stock

$^1/_2$ lb. grated Gruyère cheese

Serves six – 14.5 carb grams per serving

In a large saucepan, melt the butter or margarine and add the olive oil, onion, Sweet 'N Low,® salt and pepper. Cover with waxed paper and cook over very gentle heat, stirring frequently for about 20 minutes or until golden brown. Add the red wine and stir over moderate heat for 5 minutes or until the onions are glazed; then stir in the beef broth or stock. Bring to a boil; cover and simmer for 30 minutes. Divide the soup among four heat-proof bowls and sprinkle with cheese. Place under a hot broiler until golden brown for about 3 minutes; serve immediately.

Cream of Tomato Soup

4 tablespoons butter or margarine

2 tablespoons cooking oil

2 cups chopped onion

4 tablespoons tomato paste

8 cups chopped ripe tomatoes

1 cup dry white wine

6 cups chicken broth or stock

$^{1}/_{4}$ teaspoon Sweet 'N Low®

salt and pepper to taste

1 cup cream

Serves ten – 12.2 carb grams per serving

In a large saucepan, melt the butter or margarine; add the onion and sauté for about 5 minutes. Gradually, stir in the tomato paste and continue to cook for about 2 minutes. Add the tomatoes and wine; bring to a boil. Then add the chicken broth or stock, Sweet 'N Low,® salt and pepper. Cover and simmer, stirring occasionally for about 20 minutes. In a food processor, blend the soup until it attains a smooth consistency. Return the soup to the saucepan and stir in the cream to reheat before serving.

Fresh Watercress Soup

8 tablespoons butter or margarine

2 cups chopped onion

1^1/$_2$ teaspoons garlic, minced

4 bunches chopped watercress

4^1/$_2$ cups chicken broth or stock

salt and pepper to taste

2 cups milk

2 cups cream

4 eggs yolks, beaten

Chives, finely chopped for garnish

Serves eight – 9.4 carb grams per serving

Heat the butter or margarine in a large saucepan; sauté the onion and garlic until soft. Add the watercress; cover and cook for about 5 to 6 minutes. Then add the chicken broth or stock to the mixture and simmer for 15 to 20 minutes; allow to cool. In a food processor, blend the soup until it attains a smooth consistency. Return the mixture to the saucepan and add the seasonings. Stir in the milk, cream and egg yolks, allowing the eggs to cook; then serve and sprinkle with chives.

Chevella's Gazpacho

2 cups beef broth or stock

2 medium cucumbers, peeled and finely chopped

1 cup green onion, finely chopped

1 medium green pepper, finely chopped

2 medium tomatoes, finely chopped

2 avocados, peeled and diced

2 teaspoons garlic, minced

1 cup tomato sauce

$^1/_2$ cup water

1 tablespoon red wine vinegar

$^1/_2$ teaspoon Tabasco®

2 teaspoons Worcestershire sauce

1 teaspoon fresh parsley, finely chopped

$^1/_8$ teaspoon cayenne pepper

$^1/_8$ teaspoon salt

Serves six – 15.5 carb grams per serving

Pour the beef broth or stock into a large bowl, then gradually add each ingredient until well combined. Refrigerate for at least 4 hours; then serve in chilled bowls.

Chevellita's Tortilla Soup

$^1/_2$ cup cooking oil

2 cups chopped onion

6 teaspoons garlic, minced

2 tablespoons paprika

4 teaspoons ground cumin

2 teaspoons ground coriander

2 teaspoons chili powder

$^1/_2$ teaspoon cayenne pepper

3 quarts chicken broth or stock

6 cups canned diced tomatoes in sauce

4 bay leaves

1$^1/_2$ tablespoons salt

$^1/_2$ cup cilantro leaves plus 6 tablespoons chopped cilantro

3$^1/_2$ lbs. boneless, skinless chicken breasts, cut into $^1/_2$ inch pieces

2 avocados, peeled and diced

$^1/_2$ lb. grated Cheddar cheese

Limes, cut into quarters for garnish

Serves twelve – 12.0 carb grams per serving

In a large pot, over moderately low heat, sauté the onion, garlic and spices until soft. Add the broth, tomatoes, bay leaves, salt and $^1/_2$ cup cilantro; simmer for about 30 minutes and remove the bay leaves. Purée the soup in food processor; then return the mixture to the pot. Add the chicken to the soup and cook until done. Gently, stir in the diced avocado. To serve, sprinkle the cheese into individual bowls and pour in the soup. Garnish with remaining chopped cilantro and quartered limes.

Chilled Salmon Bisque

3 tablespoons butter or margarine

1 small onion, sliced

$^1/_2$ green pepper, finely chopped

$^1/_2$ teaspoon garlic, minced

$1^1/_2$ cups milk

1 tablespoon dill, finely chopped

4 salmon fillets, about 6 oz. each

$^3/_4$ cup cream

2 tablespoons dry sherry

$^1/_2$ teaspoon cayenne pepper

salt and white pepper to taste

Dill sprigs for garnish

Serves six – 6.3 carb grams per serving

Melt 2 tablespoons of the butter or margarine in a medium skillet and sauté the onion, green pepper and garlic until tender; remove from the heat and set aside.

In a large saucepan, heat the milk and chopped dill to just under a boil. Season the salmon fillets on both sides with salt and pepper, then poach them in the simmering milk until flaky, about 10 minutes. Transfer the salmon along with the milk to a food processor; purée until smooth. Then add the cream, remaining tablespoon of butter and sautéed vegetables continuing to purée to attain a smooth consistency. Pour the soup into a bowl; then stir in the sherry and cayenne pepper. Salt and white pepper to taste; then cover the bowl and refrigerate for 1 to 2 hours until chilled.

Spoon the salmon bisque into chilled bowls and garnish with dill sprigs.

Creamy Crab Bisque

1/4 cup butter or margarine

1 1/2 cups onion, finely chopped

6 cups cream

1 lb. crabmeat

2 tablespoons chopped fresh parsley

salt and white pepper to taste

Serves eight – 8.2 carb grams per serving

In a large saucepan, melt the butter or margarine and sauté the onion until soft. Pour in the cream and season with salt and white pepper to taste. Cook over medium heat for about 20 to 30 minutes, stirring occasionally. Add the crabmeat and parsley; cook an additional 5 to 10 minutes and then serve.

Oyster Stew

4 tablespoons butter or margarine

36 shucked oysters

1 tablespoon Worcestershire sauce

3 cups cream

1 cup milk

1/2 teaspoon salt

1/4 teaspoon white pepper

1/2 teaspoon Tabasco®

Serves six – 10.5 carb grams per serving

In a large saucepan, melt 2 tablespoons of the butter or margarine and sauté the oysters over medium-high heat until their edges begin to curl. Add the Worcestershire sauce, cream and milk. Reduce the heat and simmer for 15 to 20 minutes until the soup is hot; do not allow the liquid to reach a boil. Add the salt, white pepper, Tabasco® and remaining 2 tablespoons of butter or margarine. Enjoy!

Grandma's Seafood Gumbo

1¼ cups cooking oil

1 large white onion, finely chopped

2 stalks celery, finely chopped

5 to 6 cloves garlic, minced

½ green pepper, finely chopped

4 sprigs fresh parsley, finely chopped

2 8 oz. cans tomato sauce

1 8 oz. can whole tomatoes, mashed

2 cups water

4 lbs. fresh raw shrimp, peeled and deveined

4 hard shell crabs, broken in half

1½ lbs. chopped okra

2 bay leaves

1½ teaspoons salt

1 teaspoon black pepper

½ lb. lump crabmeat

Serves eight – 14.8 carb grams per serving

In a large pot, heat the oil and except for the okra cook all other chopped vegetables over medium heat until soft. Add the tomato sauce and the mashed whole tomatoes; simmer for a few more minutes. Then add the water, shrimp, crabs, okra, bay leaves, salt and pepper. Stir gently to mix. Cover and cook over low heat until the shrimp and okra are tender. Turn off the heat and leave the gumbo in the pot, covered. When you are ready to serve, turn the heat on low and add the lump crabmeat. Heat just until the gumbo and crabmeat are warmed. Serve immediately.

Stocks

Chicken Stock

3 lbs. chicken bones and parts

1 small onion, diced

1 celery rib, diced

1 garlic clove

3 quarts cold water

Yields 1½ quarts – 0.5 carb grams per 1 cup

Combine all ingredients in a stockpot and cover with 3 quarts cold water. Bring the stock to a boil over high heat, skimming away the residue that rises to the surface. Reduce the heat and cook at a low rolling boil until reduced by half, about 2 hours. Strain the stock and use immediately or cover and refrigerate. Chicken stock can be frozen in smaller quantities for use in a variety of recipes.

Beef Stock

1 lb. beef bones

1 small white onion, diced

1 celery rib, diced

1 garlic clove

½ bunch scallions, diced

4 quarts cold water

Preheat oven to 450° F.

Yields 2 quarts – 0.5 carb grams per 1 cup

Arrange the beef bones in a single layer in a roasting pan. Roast in a hot oven until brown, about 15 minutes, stirring the bones occasionally.

Transfer the bones to a stockpot and add the remaining ingredients. Bring the stock to a boil over high heat, skimming away the residue from the surface. Lower the heat and cook at a low rolling boil until reduced by half, about 2 hours. Strain and use immediately or freeze in smaller portions for use in a variety of recipes.

Vegetable Stock

$^3/_4$ lb. mixed vegetables and trimmings,
chopped celery, leeks, scallions, parsley

2$^1/_2$ quarts water

1 chopped onion

2 bay leaves, torn

salt and pepper to taste

Yields 2 quarts – 2.0 carb grams per 1 cup

Put all ingredients in a large pot. Add water and bring to a boil. Simmer, uncovered, for 1 hour, then drain.

Fish Stock

1$^1/_2$ quarts cold water

1 lb. fish bones and trimmings

$^1/_2$ of a lemon

$^1/_2$ cup dry white wine

Yields 3 cups – 0 carb grams per 1 cup

Bring 1$^1/_2$ quarts of cold water to a boil in a large saucepan, along with the lemon and white wine. When the water reaches a rolling boil, add the fish bones and trimmings. Lower the heat and simmer until reduced by half, about 2 hours. Drain and refrigerate, covered, for several days or freeze for future use.

Shrimp Stock

Shells and tails from 4 lbs. shrimp

8 cups water

2 cups dry white wine

3 bay leaves

6 garlic cloves

8 chopped green onions

1 cup fresh parsley, coarsely chopped

4 chopped stalks celery

1 teaspoon salt

1 teaspoon white pepper

Yields 2 quarts – 1.0 carb grams per 1 cup

Place all ingredients in a large pot; and bring to a boil. Leave uncovered and simmer for 1 hour. Strain the stock and use immediately or cover and refrigerate.

Salads

Marinated Artichoke Salad

1 1/2 cups canned artichoke hearts, drained and chopped

1 cup mushrooms, sliced

1/2 cup green olives, pitted and sliced

1/2 cup black olives, pitted and sliced

1/2 cup chopped onion

1/2 cup chopped celery

1 cup chopped tomato

Marinade:

1 cup olive oil

4 tablespoons red wine vinegar

1 teaspoon garlic, minced

1 teaspoon basil

1 teaspoon oregano

1/2 teaspoon mustard powder

salt and pepper to taste

Serves eight – 5.7 carb grams per serving

In a blender, combine all marinade ingredients and set aside. In a bowl, combine all salad ingredients and toss with the marinade. Cover and chill for 24 hours. Serve and enjoy!

Asparagus and Hearts of Palm Vinaigrette

1 lb. asparagus, par-boiled, drained and cut into 1 inch pieces

2 cups canned hearts of palm, drained and cut into $1/2$ inch slices

Vinaigrette:

$3/4$ cup olive oil

4 tablespoons red wine vinegar

2 tablespoons chopped pimento

2 teaspoons garlic, minced

$1/2$ teaspoon mustard powder

1 tablespoon dried parsley

salt and pepper to taste

Serves six – 6.2 carb grams per serving

In a blender, thoroughly combine all vinaigrette ingredients. Toss the asparagus and hearts of palm with the vinaigrette and refrigerate for 4 to 6 hours; then serve.

Avocado, Broccoli and Pecan Vinaigrette

6 cups broccoli, cut into florets

2 avocados, peeled, pitted and cut into 1 inch pieces

1 cup olive oil

6 tablespoons red wine vinegar

2 tablespoons lemon juice

1 tablespoon Dijon mustard

$3/4$ cup fresh parsley, finely chopped

$1/4$ cup chopped fresh chives

3 tablespoons shallots, finely chopped

1 cup chopped pecans

salt and pepper to taste

Serves eight – 10.1 carb grams per serving

In a saucepan, boil the broccoli in salted water for about 3 minutes or until almost tender. Drain, cool under running water, then drain again; set aside. Coat the avocado with 1 tablespoon of the lemon juice to prevent darkening. Place the avocado and broccoli in a salad bowl and gently toss in the pecans. In a small bowl, thoroughly combine all other ingredients. Pour the dressing over the salad; toss and serve immediately.

Cauliflower, Cucumber and Tomato Salad

3 cups cauliflower, par-boiled and chopped

1 cup chopped cucumber

1 cup chopped tomato

1 cup mushrooms, sliced

1 cup black olives, pitted and halved

$^1/_2$ cup red bell pepper

$^1/_2$ cup green bell pepper

$^1/_2$ cup chopped celery

$^1/_2$ cup chopped onion

Dressing:

$^1/_2$ cup red wine vinegar

1 cup olive oil

2 tablespoons chopped parsley

$^1/_2$ teaspoon garlic, minced

$^1/_2$ teaspoon salt

$^1/_4$ teaspoon black pepper

$^1/_2$ teaspoon Tabasco®

Serves six – 9.9 carb grams per serving

In a bowl, toss ingredients together well. Cover and refrigerate for 2 hours; then serve.

Broccoli and Spinach Cole Slaw

3 cups cabbage, shredded

1 cup chopped broccoli

3 cups chopped spinach

6 chopped hard-boiled eggs

1 cup mushrooms, sliced

$^{1}/_{4}$ cup chopped green pepper

$^{1}/_{4}$ cup chopped red pepper

Dressing:

1 cup mayonnaise

1 cup sour cream

$^{1}/_{4}$ cup milk

1 teaspoon dill

$^{1}/_{2}$ teaspoon garlic powder

2 tablespoons fresh lemon juice

$^{1}/_{2}$ teaspoon salt

$^{1}/_{4}$ teaspoon black pepper

Serves eight – 6.2 carb grams per serving

In a blender, thoroughly combine the dressing ingredients. Toss the salad with the dressing and chill for at least 2 hours before serving.

German Cole Slaw

1 large cabbage, shredded

2 teaspoons salt

1 teaspoon black pepper

1 medium onion, finely chopped

2 stalks celery, finely chopped

^{3}/4 cup olive oil

6 tablespoons red wine vinegar with garlic

Serves eight – 10.1 carb grams per serving

In a large serving bowl, sprinkle the cabbage with salt and pepper then add onion and celery; mix thoroughly. Add the olive oil and vinegar; mix well. Cover and refrigerate for 4 to 6 hours, stirring occasionally; then serve.

Creamy Cole Slaw

2 large heads cabbage, shredded

1 green pepper, thinly sliced

2 medium onions, thinly sliced

Dressing:

3 cups mayonnaise

2 tablespoons Dijon mustard

1 tablespoon celery seed

6 tablespoons lemon juice

^{3}/4 teaspoon granulated Sweet 'N Low®

salt and pepper to taste

Serves twelve – 12.7 carb grams per serving

In a blender, thoroughly combine all of the dressing ingredients. Toss the cabbage, green pepper and onion with the dressing; then refrigerate for 2 hours before serving.

Green Bean Salad

1 lb. green beans, par-boiled and cut in halves

$^1/_2$ onion, thinly sliced

1 cup cherry tomatoes, cut in halves

1 tablespoon red wine vinegar

2 tablespoons water

2 teaspoons olive oil

1 teaspoon basil

$^1/_4$ teaspoon dry mustard

salt and pepper to taste

Serves six – 7.7 carb grams per serving

In a bowl, toss the green beans, onion and cherry tomatoes. In a blender, thoroughly combine the remaining ingredients. Toss the vegetables with the blended dressing and refrigerate for 2 hours before serving.

Greek Tomato Salad

1 garlic clove, minced

$^1/_4$ cup green onion, finely chopped

3 cups chopped tomato

12 black olives, pitted and halved

1 cup crumbled Feta cheese

3 tablespoons red wine vinegar

$^1/_2$ cup olive oil

$^1/_2$ teaspoon oregano

$^1/_2$ teaspoon thyme

salt and pepper to taste

Serves four – 9.6 carb grams per serving

In a bowl, toss all ingredients together well. Cover and refrigerate for at least 4 hours; then serve.

Tomato, Mozzarella and Onion Salad

4 cups chopped tomato
1 cup chopped onion
1 lb. chopped Mozzarella cheese

Dressing:

1 cup olive oil
$^1/_2$ cup balsamic vinegar
$^3/_4$ teaspoon basil
salt and pepper to taste

Serves eight – 10.9 carb grams per serving

In a bowl, toss all ingredients together well. Cover and refrigerate for at least 4 hours; then serve.

Marinated Vegetable Salad

2 cups asparagus, par-boiled, drained and cut into 1 inch pieces

2 cups artichoke hearts, drained and cut in half

1 cup hearts of palm, drained and sliced

$1/2$ cup mushrooms, sliced

$1/4$ cup black olives, pitted and sliced

$1/4$ cup green olives, pitted and sliced

2 cups cherry tomatoes, halved

1 onion, sliced

whole lettuce leaves

Dressing:

1 cup olive oil

$1/2$ cup lemon juice

2 tablespoons anchovy paste

$1/2$ cup green onion, finely chopped

$1 1/2$ teaspoons garlic, minced

2 tablespoons grated Parmesan cheese

$1/4$ teaspoon salt

$1/2$ teaspoon black pepper

Serves ten – 9.7 carb grams per serving

In a blender, thoroughly combine all dressing ingredients. Toss the salad
ingredients with the dressing and chill for 24 hours before serving atop lettuce leaves.

Creamy Vegetable Salad

2 cups broccoli, par-boiled and cut into florets

2 cups cauliflower, par-boiled and cut into florets

2 cups green beans, par-boiled and cut into 1 inch pieces

2 cups celery, coarsely chopped

2 large zucchini, par-boiled and sliced

$1^{1}/_{2}$ cups mushrooms, par-boiled and sliced

1 onion, sliced

1 large green pepper, coarsely chopped

1 large red pepper, coarsely chopped

whole lettuce leaves

Dressing:

2 cups mayonnaise

4 tablespoons olive oil

$^{1}/_{2}$ cup lemon juice

$^{1}/_{2}$ teaspoon garlic, minced

1 teaspoon tarragon

2 teaspoons dill

2 tablespoons parsley, finely chopped

Serves twelve – 9.2 carb grams per serving

In a blender, thoroughly mix the dressing ingredients. In a bowl, toss the salad ingredients with the dressing and refrigerate for at least 1 hour. Serve atop lettuce leaves and enjoy!

Grecian Salad

$^{1}/_{2}$ cup cooking oil

2 cups chopped pepperoni

6 cups chopped romaine lettuce

2 cups chopped cucumber

6 tomatoes, coarsely chopped

2 onions, thinly sliced

2 green peppers, thinly sliced

2 cups black or Kalamata olives, pitted and halved

3 cups crumbled Feta cheese

Dressing:

$^{1}/_{2}$ cup lemon juice

2 teaspoons oregano

1 teaspoon garlic powder

1 teaspoon salt

$^{1}/_{2}$ teaspoon black pepper

1 cup olive oil

Serves twelve – 12.0 carb grams per serving

In a saucepan, heat the cooking oil and sauté the pepperoni until browned; then drain. In a blender, thoroughly combine the dressing ingredients. In a large salad bowl, toss the remaining salad ingredients with the dressing and pepperoni; then serve.

Italian Salad

3 cups chopped lettuce

1 cup chopped ham

1 cup chopped hard salami

1 cup chopped Mozzarella cheese

2 cups chopped tomato

1 cup marinated artichoke hearts, drained and chopped

2 cups black olives, pitted and halved

Dressing:

1 cup olive oil

$^1/_2$ cup red wine vinegar

$^1/_2$ teaspoon garlic powder

$^1/_2$ teaspoon Italian seasoning

$^1/_4$ teaspoon crushed red peppers

1 teaspoon salt

$^1/_2$ teaspoon black pepper

Serves six – 10.0 carb grams per serving

In a blender, thoroughly combine the dressing ingredients. Toss the salad with the dressing and enjoy!

93

Teddy's Caesar Salad with Chicken or Shrimp

1 medium clove garlic, minced

1 tablespoon olive oil plus $^1/_2$ cup olive oil

4 flat anchovy fillets, drained

$^1/_8$ teaspoon dry mustard

1 teaspoon Worcestershire sauce

$2^1/_2$ tablespoons red wine vinegar

juice of $^1/_2$ lemon

$^1/_4$ teaspoon salt

$^1/_2$ teaspoon black pepper

1 head romaine lettuce, cut into chunks

1 heaping tablespoon grated Parmesan cheese

4 sliced, grilled, boneless chicken breasts or 24 grilled shrimp

Serves four – 4.0 carb grams per serving

In a salad bowl, mash the garlic; gradually adding 1 tablespoon of the olive oil and anchovies until a paste is formed. Add the mustard, Worcestershire sauce, remaining olive oil, vinegar, lemon juice, salt and pepper, mixing well. Add the romaine lettuce, cheese and chicken or shrimp and toss thoroughly before serving.

Mixed Green Garlic Salad

4 cups chopped romaine lettuce

4 cups chopped iceberg lettuce

2 tablespoons grated Parmesan cheese

Dressing:

$1^1/2$ teaspoons garlic, minced

$^1/2$ teaspoon salt

$^1/4$ teaspoon black pepper

$^1/4$ teaspoon dry mustard

1 tablespoon tarragon vinegar

$^1/4$ cup olive oil

Serves six – 2.1 carb grams per serving

In a blender, thoroughly combine the dressing ingredients. In a large bowl, sprinkle the lettuce with the Parmesan cheese and toss well with the dressing. Enjoy!

Mixed Greens with Stilton and Pecan Vinaigrette

6 cups salad greens

$^1/2$ cup pecans, finely chopped

Dressing:

1 cup olive oil

6 tablespoons balsamic vinegar

$^1/2$ cup crumbled Stilton cheese

salt and pepper to taste

Serves six – 6.6 carb grams per serving

In a blender, thoroughly combine the dressing ingredients; then toss well with salad greens and pecans. Enjoy!

95

Spinach Walnut Salad

1$\frac{1}{2}$ cups spinach leaves

2 cups mushrooms, sliced

4 strips bacon, cooked crisp and crumbled

$\frac{1}{2}$ cup walnuts, finely chopped

2 chopped hard-boiled eggs

8 thin slices onion

1 cup Vinaigrette dressing (see Index)

Serves six – 9.4 carb grams per serving

In a large bowl, toss the spinach, mushrooms, bacon, walnuts and Vinaigrette dressing. Divide salad among four individual plates; garnish each salad with 2 onion slices and sprinkles of hard-boiled egg.

Roman Beef Salad

3 cups cooked roast or steak, cut into 1 inch pieces

1^1/2 cups green beans, par-boiled and cut into 1 inch pieces

1 cup mushrooms, sliced

2 medium tomatoes, cut into quarters

^{1}/2 red onion, thinly sliced

^{1}/2 cup hearts of palm, thinly sliced

^{3}/4 cup chopped green pepper

3 tablespoons chopped fresh oregano

3 tablespoons chopped fresh thyme

Dressing:

4 teaspoons capers, drained

3 teaspoons lemon juice

^{1}/2 cup red wine vinegar

1^1/2 cups olive oil

4 teaspoons Dijon mustard

^{3}/4 teaspoon salt

^{1}/4 teaspoon black pepper

Serves six – 7.7 carb grams per serving

In a blender, thoroughly combine the dressing ingredients. Use about ^{1}/3 of the dressing to marinate the beef for 2 hours before serving. Combine the marinated beef with the other salad ingredients and toss with the remaining dressing.

Spicy Beef-Broccoli Salad

3 cups broccoli, par-boiled and cut into florets

3 cups cooked roast or steak, cut into 1 inch pieces

$1^{1}/2$ cups red onion, sliced

3 cups cherry tomatoes, halved

Dressing:

$1^{1}/2$ cups mayonnaise

$^{3}/4$ cup sour cream

3 tablespoons horseradish

2 tablespoons Dijon mustard

4 tablespoons olive oil

$^{1}/2$ teaspoon salt

$^{1}/2$ teaspoon black pepper

Serves eight – 9.9 carb grams per serving

In a blender, thoroughly combine the dressing ingredients and set aside. In a large bowl, mix the remaining ingredients. Pour the dressing over the salad and toss well; serve immediately.

East Side Deli Salad

6 cups cabbage, shredded

3 cups lean corned beef, cooked and chopped

$1^{1}/2$ cups Swiss cheese, shredded

2 cups Russian dressing (see Index)

Serves eight – 7.2 carb grams per serving

In a large bowl, combine all ingredients except the dressing. Cover and chill until ready to serve; then pour dressing over salad, toss and enjoy!

Wild, Wild West Salad

6 cups iceberg lettuce, shredded

3 cups cooked lean ground beef or chicken

$1^1/2$ cups chopped tomato

1 cup Cheddar cheese, shredded

1 cup Monterey Jack cheese, shredded

$1/4$ cup black olives, pitted and sliced

$1/2$ cup chopped green onion

Dressing:

4 avocados, peeled and chopped

1 cup sour cream

2 tablespoons milk

1 cup chopped green chile peppers

1 teaspoon garlic, minced

1 teaspoon chili powder

Serves eight – 14.35 carb grams per serving

In a blender, thoroughly combine the dressing ingredients. In a salad bowl, toss the dressing with the salad ingredients; then serve.

Homemade Chicken Salad

6 boneless chicken breasts, cooked and chopped

$1/2$ cup celery, finely chopped

$1/2$ cup green pepper, finely chopped

1 cup green onion, finely chopped

1 cup mayonnaise

$1/4$ cup chopped parsley

salt and pepper to taste

Serves six – 2.9 carb grams per serving

Place the chicken in a large bowl and combine with the remaining ingredients. Mix well and chill before serving.

Bangkok Chicken Salad

5 cups chicken, cooked and chopped

$^1/_2$ cup toasted slivered almonds

$^1/_2$ cup chopped celery

$^1/_4$ cup sliced water chestnuts

2 bunches chopped watercress

$^1/_2$ cup mint, finely chopped

$^1/_2$ cup cilantro, finely chopped

2 small red onions, thinly sliced

Dressing:

2 cups mayonnaise

3 teaspoons curry powder

$1^1/_2$ tablespoons soy sauce

4 teaspoons lemon juice

$^1/_2$ teaspoon crushed red pepper

1 teaspoon granulated Sweet 'N Low®

Serves six – 9.2 carb grams per serving

In a blender, thoroughly combine the dressing ingredients. Toss the salad ingredients with the dressing and refrigerate for 2 hours before serving.

Sautéed Chicken Salad Caliente

1 cup milk

1 lemon, thinly sliced

1 cup green onion, finely chopped

3 tablespoons jalapeno chile, minced

3 tablespoons cilantro, minced

3 tablespoons ginger, minced

2 teaspoons garlic, minced

6 boneless chicken breasts, each cut into 6 pieces

Cooking oil for frying

$1^{1}/2$ teaspoons salt

$1^{1}/2$ teaspoons red pepper

12 cups salad greens

Dressing:

$^{1}/2$ cup buttermilk

4 tablespoons cooking oil

2 teaspoons jalapeno chile, minced

2 teaspoons ginger, minced

2 teaspoons lemon juice

2 teaspoons Dijon mustard

1 teaspoon garlic, minced

$^{1}/4$ teaspoon salt

$^{1}/4$ teaspoon red pepper

Serves six – 5.2 carb grams per serving

In a bowl, mix the milk, lemon slices, green onion, jalapeno, 1 tablespoon of the cilantro, ginger and garlic. Toss the chicken in the mixture; cover and marinate in the refrigerator for 4 hours.

In a blender, thoroughly combine the dressing ingredients until smooth. Cover and refrigerate. In a skillet, heat the cooking oil over medium-high heat. Sprinkle the pieces of chicken with the salt and red pepper; fry each piece of chicken on both sides until well done. Remove the chicken and allow to drain on paper towel.

In a large bowl, toss the mixed greens and chicken with the dressing; transfer to serving plates. Sprinkle with the remaining 1 tablespoon of cilantro and serve.

Raspberry and Melon Chicken Salad

4 cups cooked, boneless chicken breasts, cut into 1 inch pieces

2 cups cantaloupe, diced

$1/2$ cup raspberries plus $1/4$ cup for garnish

1 cup cucumber, thinly sliced

salt and pepper to taste

6 large lettuce leaves

Dressing:

1 cup green onion, finely chopped

6 tablespoons olive oil

6 tablespoons lime juice

1 tablespoon tarragon, minced

Serves six – 9.8 carb grams per serving

In a large bowl, whisk together the dressing ingredients until well blended. Stir in the chicken, melon, raspberries and cucumber; then salt and pepper to taste. To serve, spoon the chicken salad on top of the lettuce leaves and garnish with the remaining raspberries.

Texas Ranch Turkey Salad

4 cups cooked turkey, cut into 1 inch pieces

$1^1/2$ cups zucchini, sliced

$1^1/2$ cups squash, sliced

$1/2$ cup chopped green pepper

$1/2$ cup chopped red pepper

$1/2$ cup grated Parmesan cheese

$1^1/2$ cups Ranch dressing (see Index)

Serves four – 9.7 carb grams per serving

In a large bowl, toss the salad ingredients with the Ranch dressing. Cover and chill for at least 2 hours before serving.

Bertha's Egg Salad

8 hard-boiled eggs, peeled and chopped

2 teaspoons yellow mustard

$^3/_4$ cup mayonnaise

salt and pepper to taste

Serves six – 1.1 carb grams per serving

Thoroughly blend all the ingredients together with the eggs. Refrigerate for 2 hours before serving.

Mexican Egg Salad

4 hard-boiled eggs, peeled and chopped

$^1/_4$ cup plus 1 cup sharp Cheddar cheese, shredded

2 tablespoons chopped green onion

2 teaspoons cilantro, finely chopped

1 jalapeno chile, finely chopped

3 tablespoons mayonnaise

2 tablespoons salsa

$^1/_4$ cup sour cream

$^1/_4$ teaspoon salt

$^1/_4$ teaspoon black pepper

6 large lettuce leaves

$1^1/_2$ cups chopped tomato

2 avocados, peeled and sliced

Serves six – 9.6 carb grams per serving

In a medium bowl, combine the eggs, $^1/_4$ cup Cheddar cheese, green onion, cilantro and jalapeno. In another bowl, combine the mayonnaise, salsa, sour cream, salt and pepper; and fold into egg mixture. Place each lettuce leaf on a plate and spoon egg salad on top. Sprinkle each serving with the remaining Cheddar cheese and tomato; garnish with the sliced avocado.

Homemade Tuna Salad

2 6 oz. cans tuna fish, drained

2 tablespoons mayonnaise

3 tablespoons chopped dill pickle

Serves four – 0.4 carb grams per serving

Mix all ingredients well. Serve immediately or refrigerate.

Crabmeat and Asparagus Salad

2 cups asparagus, par-boiled and cut into 1 inch pieces

1 lb. lump crabmeat, drained

6 cups shredded lettuce

6 artichoke hearts, halved

3 hard-boiled eggs, quartered

Paprika for garnish

Dressing:

$^1/_3$ cup sour cream

$^1/_3$ cup mayonnaise

2 teaspoons Dijon mustard

2 teaspoons red wine vinegar

$^1/_2$ teaspoon tarragon

$^1/_4$ teaspoon basil

1 tablespoon chopped green onion

$^1/_2$ teaspoon horseradish

Serves six – 12.6 carb grams per serving

In a blender, thoroughly combine the dressing ingredients. Gently, toss the crabmeat and asparagus with the dressing until well coated. Divide the shredded lettuce among four to six plates; top with the crabmeat and asparagus mixture. Garnish with the artichoke hearts and hard-boiled egg; sprinkle with paprika.

Ellen's Crabmeat Salad

1 lb. lump crabmeat

Mixture:

1^1/2 cups mayonnaise

^{3}/4 cup green onion, finely chopped

^{1}/4 cup onion, finely chopped

^{1}/2 cup celery, finely chopped

^{1}/2 cup green pepper, finely chopped

6 hard-boiled eggs, peeled and chopped

^{1}/2 teaspoon garlic powder

1 teaspoon salt

^{1}/2 teaspoon black pepper

^{1}/4 teaspoon cayenne pepper

Serves six – 4.8 carb grams per serving

Thoroughly combine the mixture ingredients before gently folding in the crabmeat. Refrigerate for at least 2 hours before serving. Enjoy!

Shrimp Salad

2 cups shrimp, cooked and chopped

6 hard-boiled eggs, peeled and chopped

$^1/_2$ cup green onion, finely chopped

$^1/_4$ cup celery, finely chopped

1 tablespoon chopped parsley

2 tablespoons capers, minced

2 teaspoons fresh dill, minced

1 cup mayonnaise

1 teaspoon lemon juice

1 teaspoon Dijon mustard

$^1/_4$ teaspoon salt

$^1/_8$ teaspoon cayenne pepper

4 large lettuce leaves

Lemon slices for garnish

Serves four – 4.0 carb grams per serving

In a bowl, mix the shrimp, eggs, onion, celery, parsley, capers and dill. In another bowl, thoroughly blend together the mayonnaise, lemon juice, mustard, salt and pepper; gently fold into shrimp mixture. Place each lettuce leaf on a plate and spoon the shrimp salad on top; garnish with lemon slices.

Avocado and Shrimp Salad

4 avocados, peeled and halved

1¹/2 cups shrimp, boiled and chopped

2 cups hearts of palm, thinly sliced

3 tablespoons red wine vinegar

1 tablespoon lemon juice

¹/3 cup olive oil

¹/4 cup onion, finely chopped

1 teaspoon Dijon mustard

¹/2 teaspoon garlic powder

1 teaspoon salt

¹/2 teaspoon black pepper

Serves six – 13.6 carb grams per serving

In a bowl, thoroughly combine all of the ingredients except for the avocado, shrimp and hearts of palm. After blending, carefully add to the mixture the shrimp and hearts of palm. Fill each avocado half with the shrimp salad; then refrigerate for at least 1 hour before serving.

Seafood Salad

1 head romaine lettuce, chopped into bite-size pieces

1 cup crabmeat

1 cup shrimp, boiled and chopped

1 cup grated Parmesan cheese

1 cup Vinaigrette dressing (see Index)

4 large lettuce leaves

cherry tomatoes, optional

hard-boiled egg, optional

Serves four – 9.6 carb grams per serving

Toss the lettuce, crabmeat, shrimp and Parmesan cheese with the Vinaigrette dressing. Line four plates with the lettuce leaves and top with the seafood salad. If desired, garnish with cherry tomatoes and slices of hard-boiled egg.

Very Berry Salad

3 pints fresh strawberries

1 pint fresh blueberries

1 pint fresh blackberries

1 pint fresh raspberries

2 tablespoons orange zest, finely grated

$^{1}/_{4}$ cup fresh mint, finely chopped

4 tablespoons water

1 teaspoon granulated Sweet 'N Low®

Serves twelve – 14.5 carb grams per serving

Wash all berries and drain on paper towels. Cut stems off the strawberries and cut into halves or quarters. In a large bowl, place strawberries with blueberries, blackberries and raspberries. In another bowl, mix the orange zest, mint, water and Sweet 'N Low®; add to the berry mixture. Chill overnight before serving; stir occasionally.

Fresh Fruit Salad

1 cantaloupe

2 peaches, pitted, peeled and sliced

3 apricots, pitted, peeled and sliced

3 plums, pitted, peeled and sliced

1 cup seedless grapes

juice of 1 lemon

4 tablespoons water

1 teaspoon granulated Sweet 'N Low®

Serves ten – 14.1 carb grams per serving

From the cantaloupe, scoop out the flesh into small balls and place in a bowl. Add the peaches, apricots, plums and grapes to the bowl with the cantaloupe. In another bowl, mix the lemon juice, water and Sweet 'N Low.® Add to the fruit mixture and chill overnight before serving.

Salad Dressings

Caesar Dressing

2 garlic cloves, minced

1 cup olive oil

2 tablespoons red wine vinegar

1 tablespoon fresh lemon juice

1 teaspoon Worcestershire sauce

2 dashes Tabasco®

1 teaspoon Dijon mustard

4 to 8 anchovy fillets, minced

$^{1}/_{2}$ cup grated Parmesan cheese

salt and pepper to taste

Yields 1 cup – 0.8 carb gram per 2 Tablespoons

Blend all ingredients in a food processor until smooth.

Russian Dressing

2 cups mayonnaise

$^{1}/_{2}$ cup catsup

1 tablespoon horseradish

1 tablespoon green pepper, finely chopped

2 tablespoons onion, finely chopped

1 hard-boiled egg, peeled and finely chopped

4 teaspoons fresh parsley, finely chopped

Yields 3 cups – 1.7 carb grams per 2 Tablespoons

In a bowl, use a hand mixer or a whisk to blend together all ingredients until smooth. Refrigerate for 2 hours before using.

French Dressing

$2^{1}/2$ cups olive oil

1 cup red wine vinegar

$^{3}/4$ teaspoon Dijon mustard

4 garlic cloves, minced

juice of 1 lemon

$^{1}/4$ cup Worcestershire sauce

1 teaspoon Tabasco®

salt and pepper to taste

Yields 4 cups – 0.6 carb gram per 2 Tablespoons

Blend all ingredients in a food processor. Shake well before each use.

Blue Cheese Dressing

1 cup crumbled Blue cheese, room temperature

$^{1}/2$ cup mayonnaise

$^{1}/2$ cup cream

$^{1}/2$ cup sour cream

2 tablespoons fresh parsley, finely chopped

2 teaspoons Worcestershire sauce

2 tablespoons lemon juice

2 teaspoons onion, finely chopped

$^{1}/2$ teaspoon garlic powder

salt and pepper to taste

Yields 3 cups – 0.8 carb gram per 2 Tablespoons

In a food processor, combine all ingredients until well blended. Refrigerate for 1 hour; then serve.

Italian Dressing

$1/2$ cup grated Parmesan cheese

1 teaspoon garlic, minced

$1/4$ cup green onion, finely chopped

$1/2$ cup olive oil

$1/4$ cup tarragon vinegar

3 tablespoons lemon juice

$1/2$ cup mayonnaise

1 tablespoon Dijon mustard

1 teaspoon dill

$1/4$ teaspoon oregano

$1/4$ teaspoon thyme

$1/4$ teaspoon basil

salt and pepper to taste

Yields 1$1/2$ cups – 0.9 carb gram per 2 Tablespoons

In a food processor, combine all ingredients until smooth.

Ranch Dressing

$2/3$ cup sour cream

$2/3$ cup mayonnaise

1 cup milk

1 tablespoon onion, finely chopped

2 tablespoons green onion, finely chopped

1 tablespoon garlic, minced

salt and pepper to taste

Yields 2$1/2$ cups – 1.2 carb grams per 2 Tablespoons

Whisk together all of the ingredients and refrigerate. Serve when chilled.

Green Goddess Dressing

2 cups mayonnaise

$^1/_4$ cup red wine vinegar

$^1/_4$ cup green onion, finely chopped

$^1/_4$ cup parsley, finely chopped

2 tablespoons tarragon, finely chopped

8 anchovy fillets, finely chopped

2 scallions, cut into 2 inch pieces

Yields 3 cups – 0.4 carb gram per 2 Tablespoons

In a food processor, blend all of the ingredients except for the anchovies and scallions. When mixture is blended well, add the anchovies and scallions; blend for no longer than 2 minutes, then serve.

Cobb Salad Dressing

$2^1/_2$ cups olive oil

8 tablespoons tarragon vinegar

6 tablespoons lemon juice

5 garlic cloves, minced

2 tablespoons Dijon mustard

salt and pepper to taste

$^1/_2$ cup bacon, cooked crisp and crumbled

$^1/_2$ cup chopped tomato

$^1/_2$ cup chopped avocado

$^1/_2$ cup crumbled Blue cheese

Yields 7 cups – 0.5 carb gram per 2 Tablespoons

Except for the bacon, tomato, avocado and Blue cheese, blend all other ingredients in a food processor until smooth. Pour into a bowl and gently fold in the remaining ingredients. Toss with mixed greens and bite-size pieces of chicken.

Balsamic Vinaigrette

$^2/_3$ cup balsamic vinegar

$1^1/_3$ cups olive oil

$^1/_2$ teaspoon garlic, minced

2 tablespoons lime juice

$1^1/_2$ teaspoons basil

$^1/_4$ teaspoon paprika

salt and pepper to taste

Yields 2 cups – 2.5 carb grams per 2 Tablespoons

In a food processor, blend all ingredients until smooth.

Classical Vinaigrette

2 teaspoons garlic, minced

1 teaspoon Dijon mustard

$^1/_2$ teaspoon dry mustard

5 tablespoons red wine vinegar

1 teaspoon lemon juice

4 tablespoons olive oil

1 cup cooking oil

2 teaspoons salt

1 teaspoon white pepper

$^1/_2$ teaspoon black pepper

Yields $1^1/_2$ cups – 0.4 carb gram per 2 Tablespoons

In a food processor, blend all ingredients until smooth.

Blue Cheese and Green Onion Vinaigrette

2 green onions, finely chopped

2 garlic cloves, minced

3 cups olive oil

1 cup balsamic vinegar

1 cup Blue cheese, crumbled

2 tablespoons rosemary

1 teaspoon paprika

1 teaspoon salt

1 teaspoon black pepper

Yields 5 cups – 1.7 carb grams per 2 Tablespoons

In a bowl, use a hand mixer or a whisk to blend together all of the ingredients, except for the Blue cheese until smooth. Gradually, fold the Blue cheese into the mixture and stir vigorously. Refrigerate for 2 hours before serving.

Créole Vinaigrette

1 medium onion, finely chopped

2 tablespoons garlic, minced

1 cup Créole mustard

$1/4$ cup olive oil

$1/2$ cup red wine vinegar

salt and pepper to taste

Yields $2^1/2$ cups – 1.0 carb gram per 2 Tablespoons

In a food processor, blend all ingredients until smooth.

115

Pecan Vinaigrette

2 cups olive oil

$^2/3$ cup red wine vinegar

$^1/2$ cup green onion, finely chopped

$^1/2$ cup parsley, finely chopped

2 tablespoons capers, drained and minced

2 tablespoons thyme

salt and pepper to taste

$^1/2$ cup chopped pecans

Yields 2$^1/2$ cups – 1.0 carb gram per 2 Tablespoons

In a bowl, use a hand mixer or a whisk to blend together all of the ingredients, except for the pecans, until smooth. Gradually, fold the pecans into the mixture and stir vigorously. Refrigerate for 2 hours before serving.

Spicy Oriental Vinaigrette

2 garlic cloves, minced

1$^1/2$ cups olive oil

$^1/4$ cup red wine vinegar

3 tablespoons lemon juice

1 tablespoon Chinese mustard

2 tablespoons soy sauce

4 teaspoons ginger

$^1/4$ teaspoon cayenne pepper

Yields 2 cups – 0.7 carb gram per 2 Tablespoons

In a food processor, blend all ingredients until smooth.

Creamy Garlic Dressing

2 cups sour cream

$^1/_2$ cup mayonnaise

4 garlic cloves, minced

2 green onions, finely chopped

3 teaspoons parsley, finely chopped

1 teaspoon dill

$^1/_2$ teaspoon Worcestershire sauce

salt and pepper to taste

Yields 3 cups – 1.1 carb grams per 2 Tablespoons

In a food processor, blend all ingredients until smooth.

Horseradish Dressing

2 cups sour cream

$^1/_2$ cup mayonnaise

$^1/_2$ cup green onion, finely chopped

1 teaspoon garlic, minced

2 tablespoons horseradish

2 tablespoons red wine vinegar

salt and pepper to taste

Yields 3 cups – 1.2 carb grams per 2 Tablespoons

In a food processor, blend all ingredients until smooth.

Peppercorn Parmesan Dressing

2 cups mayonnaise

3 tablespoons Dijon mustard

$^1/_2$ cup Parmesan cheese

2 tablespoons milk

1 tablespoon red wine vinegar

1 tablespoon lemon juice

1 tablespoon garlic, minced

1 teaspoon black pepper, coarsely ground

Yields 2 $^1/_2$ cups – 0.6 carb gram per 2 Tablespoons

In a small bowl, use a hand mixer or whisk together all ingredients until smooth. Add more milk for a thinner consistency. Chill before serving.

Mayonnaise

Homemade Mayonnaise

2 egg yolks

1 teaspoon lemon juice

$^1/_2$ teaspoon dry mustard

$^1/_2$ teaspoon salt

pinch of cayenne pepper

2 cups cooking or olive oil

2 tablespoons boiling water

Yields 2 $^1/_4$ cups – 0.1 carb gram per 2 Tablespoons

In a food processor, combine the first 5 ingredients for about 3 to 5 minutes. Add 1 cup of the oil, a teaspoon at a time, until the mixture becomes a thick emulsion. Add the remaining 1 cup of oil, 1 to 2 tablespoons at a time. When all of the oil is incorporated, beat in the boiling water. Cover and refrigerate until ready to use.

Créole Mayonnaise

2 tablespoons green onion, finely chopped

2 tablespoons parsley, finely chopped

$^1/_2$ teaspoon garlic, minced

juice of 1 small lemon or lime

1 teaspoon Tabasco®

$^1/_4$ cup Créole mustard

$^3/_4$ cup mayonnaise

2 egg whites

Yields 1$^1/_2$ cups – 0.5 carb gram per 2 Tablespoons

In a food processor, except for the egg whites, thoroughly combine all other ingredients. In another bowl, whip the egg whites until thick. Using a whisk, gently fold the egg whites into the mayonnaise. Cover and chill the mayonnaise until serving.

Dijon Mayonnaise

2 egg yolks

1 teaspoon lemon juice

1 1/2 tablespoons Dijon mustard

1/2 teaspoon salt

pinch of cayenne pepper

2 cups cooking or olive oil

2 tablespoons boiling water

Yields 2 1/4 cups – 0.1 carb gram per 2 Tablespoons

In a food processor, combine the first 5 ingredients for about 3 to 5 minutes. Add 1 cup of the oil, a teaspoon at a time, until the mixture becomes a thick emulsion. Add the remaining 1 cup of oil, 1 to 2 tablespoons at a time. When all of the oil is incorporated, beat in the boiling water. Cover and refrigerate until ready to use.

Garlic Herb Mayonnaise

2 egg yolks

1 teaspoon lemon juice

2 teaspoons basil

2 teaspoons garlic powder

1/2 teaspoon dry mustard

1/2 teaspoon salt

pinch of cayenne pepper

2 cups cooking or olive oil

2 tablespoons boiling water

Yields 2 1/2 cups – 0.4 carb gram per 2 Tablespoons

In a food processor, combine the first 7 ingredients for about 3 to 5 minutes. Add 1 cup of the oil, a teaspoon at a time, until the mixture becomes a thick emulsion. Add the remaining 1 cup of oil, 1 to 2 tablespoons at a time. When all of the oil is incorporated, beat in the boiling water. Cover and refrigerate until ready to use.

Mexican Mayonnaise

2 egg yolks

6 jalapeno peppers, finely chopped

4 green onions, finely chopped

4 tablespoons cilantro, finely chopped

1 teaspoon lime juice

$1/2$ teaspoon chili powder

$1/2$ teaspoon dry mustard

$1/2$ teaspoon salt

pinch of cayenne pepper

2 cups cooking or olive oil

2 tablespoons boiling water

Yields 3 cups – 1.3 carb grams per 2 Tablespoons

In a food processor, combine the first 9 ingredients for about 3 to 5 minutes.
Add 1 cup of the oil, a teaspoon at a time, until the mixture becomes a thick emulsion.
Add the remaining 1 cup of oil, 1 to 2 tablespoons at a time. When all of the oil is
incorporated, beat in the boiling water. Cover and refrigerate until ready to use.

Oriental Mayonnaise

2 egg yolks

3 tablespoons soy sauce

$1 1/2$ tablespoons ginger, finely chopped

3 green onions, finely chopped

2 tablespoons cilantro, finely chopped

1 teaspoon lemon juice

$1/2$ teaspoon dry mustard

$1/2$ teaspoon salt

pinch of cayenne pepper

2 cups cooking or olive oil

2 tablespoons boiling water

Yields 3 cups – 0.4 carb gram per 2 Tablespoons

In a food processor, combine the first 9 ingredients for about 3 to 5 minutes.
Add 1 cup of the oil, a teaspoon at a time, until the mixture becomes a thick emulsion.
Add the remaining 1 cup of oil, 1 to 2 tablespoons at a time. When all of the oil is
incorporated, beat in the boiling water. Cover and refrigerate until ready to use.

Omelettes, Frittatas and Quiches

Basic Omelette

4 large eggs

$^1/_4$ teaspoon salt

$^1/_8$ teaspoon black pepper

3 tablespoons butter or margarine

Serves two – 1.3 carb grams per serving

In a small bowl, beat the eggs, salt and pepper with a fork until blended. Melt the butter or margarine in an 8 inch skillet or omelette pan. Pour in the egg mixture and stir briskly. Cook the eggs over low heat; lift the edges of the omelette and shake the pan several times during cooking to keep the eggs from sticking. When the eggs are firm and the bottom is light brown, fold the omelette over and transfer it to a plate.

Reuben Omelette

4 large eggs

$^1/_4$ teaspoon salt

$^1/_8$ teaspoon black pepper

3 tablespoons butter or margarine

$^3/_4$ cup chopped corned beef

$^3/_4$ cup shredded Swiss cheese

Serves two – 2.7 carb grams per serving

In a small bowl, beat the eggs, salt and pepper with a fork until blended. Melt the butter or margarine in an 8 inch skillet or omelette pan, then add the egg mixture and corned beef, stirring briskly. Cook the mixture over low heat; lift the edges of the omelette and shake the pan several times during cooking to keep the eggs from sticking. When the eggs are almost set, fold in the cheese. Cook until the bottom forms a golden crust, then fold the omelette over and transfer it to a plate.

Tex-Mex Omelette

3 tablespoons cooking oil

$^1/_4$ cup chopped green onion

$^1/_4$ cup chopped onion

$^1/_4$ cup chopped green pepper

$^1/_2$ cup chopped tomato

1 teaspoon cilantro, finely chopped

4 large eggs

$^1/_4$ teaspoon chili powder

$^1/_4$ teaspoon salt

$^1/_8$ teaspoon black pepper

3 tablespoons butter or margarine

1 avocado, pitted, peeled and sliced

$^1/_4$ cup sour cream

Serves four – 8.1 carb grams per serving

In a saucepan, heat the cooking oil over medium heat and sauté the onions, green pepper, tomato and cilantro until soft; then set aside. In a small bowl, beat the eggs, chili powder, salt and pepper with a fork until blended. Melt the butter or margarine in an 8 inch skillet or omelette pan, then add the egg mixture, stirring briskly. Cook the mixture over low heat; lift the edges of the omelette and shake the pan several times during cooking to keep the eggs from sticking. When the eggs are almost set, fold in the vegetable mixture. Cook until the bottom forms a golden crust, then fold the omelette over and transfer it to a plate. Garnish with avocado slices and sour cream.

Mushroom and Herb Omelette

4 large eggs

$^1/_2$ teaspoon salt

$^1/_8$ teaspoon black pepper

3 tablespoons butter or margarine

2 tablespoons green onion, finely chopped

1 tablespoon oregano, finely chopped

1 tablespoon parsley, finely chopped

$^3/_4$ cup mushrooms, sliced

Serves two – 3.3 carb grams per serving

In a small bowl, beat the eggs, salt and pepper with a fork until blended. Melt the butter or margarine in an 8 inch skillet or omelette pan and sauté the onion, oregano, parsley and mushrooms until soft. Pour in the egg mixture and stir briskly. Cook the eggs over low heat; lift the edges of the omelette and shake the pan several times during cooking to keep the eggs from sticking. When the eggs are firm and the bottom is light brown, fold the omelette over and transfer it to a plate.

Smoked Salmon Omelette

4 large eggs

$^1/_4$ teaspoon salt

$^1/_8$ teaspoon black pepper

3 tablespoons butter or margarine

$^1/_4$ cup chopped onion

$^3/_4$ cup chopped smoked salmon

$^1/_2$ cup sour cream

1 tablespoon parsley, finely chopped for garnish

Serves two – 5.6 carb grams per serving

In a small bowl, beat the eggs, salt and pepper with a fork until blended. Melt the butter or margarine in an 8 inch skillet or omelette pan and sauté the onion until soft. Add the smoked salmon; then pour in the egg mixture and stir briskly. Cook the eggs over low heat; lift the edges of the omelette and shake the pan several times during cooking to keep the eggs from sticking. When the eggs are firm and the bottom is light brown, fold the omelette over and transfer it to a plate. Spoon the sour cream on top and garnish with the parsley.

Broccoli and Gruyère Frittata

$^1/_2$ cup chopped onion

$^1/_2$ teaspoon garlic, minced

2 tablespoons butter or margarine

1 tablespoon olive oil

$1^1/_2$ cups broccoli, cooked and chopped

6 eggs

$^1/_2$ teaspoon salt

$^1/_4$ teaspoon black pepper

$^3/_4$ cup plus 2 tablespoons shredded Gruyère cheese

Heat the broiler

Serves six – 3.1 carb grams per serving

In an oven-proof skillet, melt the butter or margarine and oil over medium heat; sauté the onion and garlic until soft. Stir in the broccoli and remove from the heat. In a separate bowl, beat the eggs with the salt and pepper; then stir in the $^3/_4$ cup of cheese until well mixed. Pour the egg mixture over the broccoli; cover and cook over medium-low heat for about 10 minutes. Place the skillet under the broiler and heat until golden brown. Sprinkle with remaining cheese before serving.

Chicken and Asparagus Frittata

$^{1}/_{2}$ cup chopped green onion

$^{1}/_{2}$ teaspoon garlic, minced

2 tablespoons butter or margarine

1 tablespoon olive oil

1 cup chicken, cooked and chopped

1 cup asparagus, cooked and chopped

8 eggs

$^{1}/_{2}$ teaspoon salt

$^{1}/_{8}$ teaspoon cayenne pepper

2 tablespoons grated Parmesan cheese for garnish

1 tablespoon parsley, finely chopped for garnish

Heat the broiler

Serves six – 3.2 carb grams per serving

In an oven-proof skillet, melt the butter or margarine and oil over medium heat; sauté the green onion and garlic until soft. Stir in the chicken and asparagus; remove from the heat. In a separate bowl, beat the eggs with the salt and cayenne pepper. Pour the egg mixture over the chicken and asparagus; cover and cook over medium-low heat for about 10 minutes. Place the skillet under the broiler and heat until golden brown. Sprinkle with Parmesan cheese and parsley for garnish.

Hot Sausage Frittata

$^1/_2$ cup chopped onion

$^1/_2$ teaspoon garlic, minced

2 tablespoons butter or margarine

1 tablespoon olive oil

$1^1/_2$ cups hot sausage, cooked and chopped

6 eggs

$^1/_2$ teaspoon salt

$^3/_4$ cup plus 2 tablespoons shredded Cheddar cheese

Heat the broiler

Serves six – 2.9 carb grams per serving

In an oven-proof skillet, melt the butter or margarine and oil over medium heat; sauté the onion and garlic until soft. Stir in the sausage and remove from the heat. In a separate bowl, beat the eggs with the salt; then stir in the $^3/_4$ cup of cheese until well mixed. Pour the egg mixture over the sausage; cover and cook over medium-low heat for about 10 minutes. Place the skillet under the broiler and heat until golden brown. Sprinkle with remaining cheese before serving.

Crustless Quiche Lorraine

1 tablespoon butter or margarine

2 tablespoons chopped onion

2 tablespoons chopped celery

2 tablespoons chopped green pepper

12 bacon strips, cooked crisp and crumbled

4 eggs, beaten

1 cup cream

$^1/_2$ teaspoon salt

1 cup shredded Swiss cheese

Preheat oven to 350° F.

Serves four – 4.2 carb grams per serving

In a saucepan, melt the butter or margarine over medium heat and sauté the onion, celery and green pepper until soft. Add the bacon and cook for only 1 minute; then remove from fire. In a separate bowl, blend the eggs, cream and salt. Grease a 9 inch pie pan and cover the bottom with the bacon pieces and sautéed seasoning mixture. Next, sprinkle the cheese evenly over this layer; then pour in the egg mixture. Bake for 45 minutes; allow to cool slightly before serving.

Crustless Florentine Quiche

1 tablespoon butter or margarine

2 tablespoons chopped onion

2 tablespoons chopped celery

2 tablespoons chopped green pepper

1$\frac{1}{2}$ cups spinach, cooked and chopped

4 eggs, beaten

1 cup cream

$\frac{1}{2}$ teaspoon salt

1 cup shredded Mozzarella cheese

Preheat oven to 350° F.

Serves four – 4.3 carb grams per serving

In a saucepan, melt the butter or margarine over medium heat and sauté the onion, celery and green pepper until soft. Add the spinach and cook until well heated; then remove from fire. In a separate bowl, blend the eggs, cream and salt. Grease a 9 inch pie pan and cover the bottom with the sautéed seasoning mixture. Next, sprinkle the cheese evenly over this layer; then pour in the egg mixture. Bake for 45 minutes; allow to cool slightly before serving.

131

Crustless Crabmeat Quiche

1 tablespoon butter or margarine

2 tablespoons chopped onion

2 tablespoons chopped celery

2 tablespoons chopped green pepper

1 1/2 cups crabmeat

4 eggs, beaten

1 cup cream

1/2 teaspoon salt

1 cup shredded Cheddar cheese

Preheat oven to 350° F.

Serves four – 4.3 carb grams per serving

In a saucepan, melt the butter or margarine over medium heat and sauté the onion, celery and green pepper until soft. Add the crabmeat and cook until well heated; then remove from fire. In a separate bowl, blend the eggs, cream and salt. Grease a 9 inch pie pan and cover the bottom with the sautéed seasoning mixture. Next, sprinkle the cheese evenly over this layer; then pour in the egg mixture. Bake for 45 minutes; allow to cool slightly before serving.

Entrées

Crabmeat Au Gratin

1 large onion, finely chopped

4 green onions, finely chopped

$^1/_2$ cup chopped celery

1 cup butter or margarine

2 cups cream

4 cups crabmeat

$1^1/_2$ cups plus 4 tablespoons grated Cheddar cheese

4 egg yolks

3 dashes Tabasco®

Preheat oven to 350° F.

Serves four – 11.5 carb grams per serving

In a medium-sized saucepan, melt the butter or margarine and sauté the onion and celery until soft. Add the cream and blend well. Remove from heat and add all remaining ingredients, except for the 4 tablespoons of grated Cheddar cheese. Divide the crabmeat mixture among four individual casserole dishes. Sprinkle tops with remaining Cheddar cheese and bake until golden brown.

Crabmeat Imperial

2 cups crabmeat

$^1/_2$ cup green onion, finely chopped

$^1/_2$ cup green pepper, finely chopped

$^1/_4$ cup chopped pimento

1 egg yolk

1 teaspoon dry mustard

2 tablespoons paprika

salt and pepper to taste

1 cup mayonnaise

$^1/_4$ cup grated Parmesan cheese

Paprika for garnish

Preheat oven to 375° F.

Serves four – 6.2 carb grams per serving

In a large bowl, combine the crabmeat, green onion, green pepper, pimento, egg yolk, dry mustard, paprika and $^1/_2$ cup of the mayonnaise. Stir until well mixed, then season with salt and pepper. Spoon the mixture into 4 small baking dishes; then cover with the remaining mayonnaise. Sprinkle with the Parmesan cheese and bake in oven for 15 to 20 minutes. Sprinkle with paprika and serve immediately.

Barbecued Shrimp

5 lbs. jumbo raw whole shrimp, washed

4 teaspoons garlic, minced

1 tablespoon Tabasco®

2 cups butter or margarine

1¹/₂ tablespoons black pepper

2 tablespoons Worcestershire sauce

1 tablespoon cayenne pepper

juice of 4 lemons

1 tablespoon lemon zest

Preheat oven to 350° F.

Serves four – 6.3 carb grams per serving

In a large pan, melt the butter or margarine and add all the ingredients, except for the shrimp. Cook the mixture over a low fire until well blended. Place the shrimp in a large baking pan, pour the mixture over the shrimp and place in the oven for 20 minutes. With a large spoon, turn the shrimp and bake another 15 minutes before serving.

Singing Shrimp

¹/₂ cup butter or margarine

¹/₂ cup chopped onion

¹/₄ cup garlic, minced

1 cup fresh mushrooms, sliced

2 cups spicy smoked sausage, sliced

2 lbs. raw shrimp, peeled and deveined

¹/₂ cup chopped green onion

1 tablespoon chopped parsley

¹/₂ cup white wine

salt and pepper to taste

Serves four – 10.3 carb grams per serving

In a large skillet, melt the butter or margarine and sauté the onion and garlic until soft. Add the mushrooms and cook the mixture for 3 to 4 minutes. Stir in the sausage, shrimp and green onion; sauté for an additional 4 minutes before adding the parsley and white wine. Salt and pepper to taste; reduce heat and simmer briefly before serving.

Shrimp Diane

1 medium onion, finely chopped

4 garlic cloves, minced

2 stalks celery, finely chopped

$^{1}/_{4}$ cup plus 2 tablespoons parsley, finely chopped

$^{1}/_{2}$ teaspoon tarragon

2 tablespoons fresh lemon juice

$^{3}/_{4}$ cup Worcestershire sauce

$^{1}/_{4}$ teaspoon Tabasco®

2 lbs. jumbo raw shrimp, peeled and deveined

Serves six – 11.3 carb grams per serving

In a saucepan, sauté the onion, garlic, celery and $^{1}/_{4}$ cup parsley for 3 to 4 minutes; add the tarragon, lemon juice, Worcestershire sauce and Tabasco,® cooking until very hot. Add the shrimp to the mixture and cook until the shrimp are done or turn pink. Sprinkle with parsley and serve.

Asian Shrimp

1 cup cooking oil

1 cup green onion, finely chopped

2 tablespoons garlic, minced

2 tablespoons plus 1 teaspoon ginger, minced

2 teaspoons soy sauce

1 teaspoon Chinese mustard

$^{1}/_{2}$ cup chicken broth or stock

3 lbs. raw shrimp, peeled and deveined

salt and pepper to taste

Serves six – 4.9 carb grams per serving

In a saucepan, sauté the onion, garlic and ginger until brown. Pour in the soy sauce, mustard and broth or stock and bring to a boil. Turn off the heat and add the shrimp, thoroughly tossing with the seasoned mixture. Cover and refrigerate for at least 3 hours, stirring occasionally. Remove from refrigerator and return to a large saucepan for heating. Cook the shrimp over medium-high heat for about 5 to 7 minutes. Salt and pepper to taste; then serve.

Italian Shrimp

1 cup olive oil

¹/₂ cup chopped green pepper

1 cup chopped onion

1 tablespoon garlic, minced

1¹/₂ cups mushrooms, sliced

29 oz. canned tomatoes, mashed

3 tablespoons red wine vinegar

1 teaspoon Italian seasoning

¹/₂ teaspoon cayenne pepper

2 lbs. raw shrimp, peeled and deveined

¹/₂ cup grated Parmesan cheese

2 teaspoons paprika

Serves six – 12.6 carb grams per serving

In a saucepan, heat the olive oil and sauté the green pepper, onion and garlic until soft. Add the mushrooms, tomatoes, vinegar and Italian seasoning and simmer over medium-low heat for about 10 minutes. Reduce the heat to low and add the shrimp with the cayenne pepper. Allow to simmer for an additional 10 minutes or until the shrimp are pink and completely cooked. Sprinkle with Parmesan cheese and paprika before serving.

Florentine Shrimp

20 oz. frozen chopped spinach, cooked and drained

$^{1}/_{2}$ teaspoon garlic powder

$^{1}/_{4}$ teaspoon salt

$^{1}/_{4}$ teaspoon black pepper

$^{1}/_{4}$ cup butter or margarine

2 tablespoons garlic, minced

2 lbs. raw shrimp, peeled and deveined

$^{1}/_{2}$ cup bacon, cooked crisp and crumbled

$^{1}/_{2}$ teaspoon Tabasco®

$^{1}/_{4}$ teaspoon crushed red pepper

Serves four – 9.6 carb grams per serving

Season the cooked spinach with the garlic powder, salt and pepper; cover to keep warm. Sauté the garlic in the butter or margarine until light brown. Add the shrimp and allow shrimp to cook until done or pink. Stir in the bacon, Tabasco® and red pepper. Then arrange the spinach on a serving platter and spoon the shrimp mixture on top before serving.

Scallops Créole

4 teaspoons olive oil

1 cup onion, finely chopped

1 cup green pepper, finely chopped

4 teaspoons garlic, minced

4 cups tomato, coarsely chopped

$^1/_2$ cup tomato paste

1 teaspoon basil

$^1/_2$ teaspoon thyme

$^1/_2$ teaspoon crushed red pepper

$^1/_4$ teaspoon oregano

20 oz. bay scallops

Serves six – 15.9 carb grams per serving

In a large skillet, heat the olive oil and sauté the onion, green pepper and garlic until soft. Stir in remaining ingredients, except for the scallops. Reduce heat to medium-low and cook for 5 minutes. Add the scallops and cook for an additional 4 minutes or until done. Serve immediately.

Sautéed Scallops

2 tablespoons butter or margarine

4 cups fresh mushrooms, sliced

2 cups onion, finely chopped

2 teaspoons garlic, minced

2 tablespoons lime juice

1 teaspoon thyme

1 teaspoon lemon pepper marinade

20 oz. bay scallops

Serves four – 14.5 carb grams per serving

In a large skillet, melt the butter or margarine and sauté the mushrooms, onion and garlic until soft. Stir in remaining ingredients and cook until scallops are done; serve immediately.

Mussels Milano

2 tablespoons olive oil
2 tablespoons butter or margarine
4 garlic cloves, minced
1 cup onion, finely chopped
2 tablespoons parsley, finely chopped
4 basil leaves, finely chopped
$^1/_2$ teaspoon oregano
2 teaspoons black pepper
36 fresh mussels, cleaned
1 cup dry white wine

Serves four – 11.2 carb grams per serving

In a large pot, combine the olive oil, butter or margarine, garlic, onion, parsley, basil, oregano and pepper. Stir and heat gently for 10 minutes; add the mussels and wine. Cover, bring to a boil and allow to simmer until the shells open. Before serving, remove any mussels that do not open. Enjoy!

Citrus Salmon with Caper Butter

1 cup butter or margarine
6 tablespoons parsley, minced
4 garlic cloves, minced
4 tablespoons capers, drained
1 tablespoon lemon juice
1 tablespoon grated lemon zest
1 teaspoon salt
$^1/_2$ teaspoon white pepper
6 salmon steaks, 6 to 8 oz. each
2 tablespoons olive oil
Preheat oven to 350° F.

Serves six – 1.7 carb grams per serving

With a hand mixer, carefully blend the butter or margarine, parsley, garlic, capers, lemon juice, zest, $^1/_4$ teaspoon salt and $^1/_4$ teaspoon pepper; then set mixture aside. Baste the salmon with the olive oil and season with the remaining salt and pepper. Bake the salmon for about 15 to 20 minutes or until done. Spread the lemon-caper butter evenly atop the salmon and allow to melt before serving.

Salmon with Creamy Mustard Sauce

4 salmon fillets, 8 oz. each

4 tablespoons sour cream

2 tablespoons Dijon mustard

2 teaspoons lemon pepper seasoning

Heat the broiler

Serves four – 1.4 carb grams per serving

Place the salmon on a lightly greased broiler pan. Broil for 8 to 12 minutes, turning once half of the broiling time. In a small bowl, stir together the sour cream, mustard and seasoning. Spread the mixture over the salmon and broil until creamy mustard sauce is lightly browned.

Dill-Topped Salmon Steaks

4 tablespoons butter or margarine

1 cup cream

$^3/_4$ cup dry white wine

2 tablespoons lemon juice

2 tablespoons dill, finely chopped

4 salmon steaks, 8 oz. each

Serves four – 2.7 carb grams per serving

In a large skillet, melt the butter or margarine over high heat. Add all the ingredients, except for the salmon; stir well. Add the salmon and reduce the heat to medium-low. Simmer for about 8 minutes, then turn salmon and cook for an additional 8 minutes. Place the salmon steaks on a platter; top with dill sauce and serve.

Red Snapper with Herb Butter

4 tablespoons butter or margarine, room temperature

2 teaspoons lemon or lime juice

1 teaspoon lemon or lime zest

$^1/_4$ teaspoon garlic, minced

$^1/_2$ teaspoon tarragon, finely chopped

$^1/_2$ teaspoon rosemary, finely chopped

$^1/_2$ teaspoon black pepper

4 red snapper steaks, 6 to 8 oz. each

2 teaspoons butter or margarine, melted

$^1/_4$ cup parsley, finely chopped

Heat the broiler

Serves four – 0.8 carb gram per serving

In a small bowl, mix together the 4 tablespoons butter or margarine, lemon or lime juice, zest, garlic, tarragon, rosemary and black pepper; set aside. Place the red snapper on a lightly greased broiler pan; baste with the 2 teaspoons of melted butter or margarine. Broil 4 to 6 minutes, then turn and broil for an additional 4 to 6 minutes. Spread the herb butter mixture evenly atop each red snapper steak; allow to melt before serving. Sprinkle with parsley for garnish.

Blackened Fish Boutte

2 teaspoons garlic powder

2 teaspoons oregano

1 teaspoon chili powder

1 teaspoon thyme

$^1/_2$ teaspoon Tabasco®

$^1/_2$ teaspoon cayenne pepper

$^1/_2$ teaspoon black pepper

6 fish fillets, 6 to 8 oz. each

$^1/_2$ cup butter or margarine

$^1/_4$ cup olive oil

2 lemons, cut into quarters for garnish

Serves six – 1.6 carb grams per serving

Thoroughly combine the first 7 ingredients in a bowl. Rub the mixture on both sides of the fish fillets, then heat the butter or margarine and olive oil in a large skillet over high heat. When oil becomes very hot, cook the fish fillets for 3 to 4 minutes on each side or until done. Serve with lemon for garnish.

Herbed-Flounder Meunière

$^1/_2$ cup butter or margarine

1 teaspoon dill

1 teaspoon thyme

$^1/_2$ teaspoon garlic, minced

2 green onions, thinly sliced

2 tablespoons lemon juice

4 Flounder fillets, 6 to 8 oz. each

Serves four – 1.5 carb grams per serving

In a large skillet, melt the butter or margarine and sauté the dill, thyme, garlic, green onion and lemon juice. Add the Flounder fillets and cook over medium heat for 4 to 6 minutes on each side or until brown. Place the fillets on a serving platter; pour the herbed butter sauce over the Flounder and serve.

Southern Baked Halibut

$^1/_2$ tablespoon olive oil

$^1/_2$ cup chopped tomato

$^1/_4$ cup onion, finely chopped

$^1/_4$ cup green pepper, finely chopped

$^1/_4$ cup celery, finely chopped

$^3/_4$ teaspoon oregano, finely chopped

$^1/_2$ teaspoon basil, finely chopped

$^1/_2$ teaspoon thyme, finely chopped

$^1/_4$ teaspoon white pepper

$^1/_4$ teaspoon cayenne pepper

$^1/_4$ teaspoon black pepper

$^1/_4$ teaspoon paprika

$^3/_4$ cup chicken broth or stock

4 Halibut fillets, 6 to 8 oz. each

Cooking spray

4 tablespoons parsley, finely chopped

Preheat oven to 375° F.

Serves four – 3.6 carb grams per serving

In a large skillet, heat the olive oil over medium heat and add the tomato, onion, celery, green pepper, garlic and seasonings, stirring thoroughly to combine; sauté until soft. Stir in the broth or stock and bring to a boil. Reduce heat and simmer, stirring occasionally until the vegetables are tender for about 20 minutes.

Place the Halibut fillets in a baking dish, sprayed with cooking spray. Pour the sauce over the Halibut fillets and bake, uncovered, for about 20 minutes or until fish is tender. When ready to serve, place fillets on a platter and top with the sauce. Sprinkle with parsley for garnish.

Cajun Tuna

1 cup butter or margarine, room temperature

2 teaspoons chili powder

1 teaspoon Tabasco®

$^1/_2$ teaspoon crushed red pepper

$^1/_2$ teaspoon salt

4 tuna steaks, 6 to 8 oz. each

$^1/_4$ cup olive oil

salt and pepper to taste

Heat the broiler

Serves four – 0.7 carb gram per serving

In a small bowl, mix butter or margarine, chili powder, Tabasco,® red pepper and the $^1/_2$ teaspoon salt. Rub each tuna steak lightly with the olive oil and sprinkle with additional salt and pepper. Place the tuna steaks in a broiling pan and cook for about 10 to 12 minutes on each side. Remove the steaks and place on serving plates. Top each tuna steak with $^1/_4$ of the spicy butter; allow to melt before serving.

Tuna Capri

$^1/_2$ cup olive oil

1 cup chopped onion

2 teaspoons garlic, minced

1 cup black olives, pitted and chopped

3 tablespoons red wine vinegar

1 teaspoon lemon juice

1 teaspoon oregano

$^1/_2$ teaspoon salt

$^1/_2$ teaspoon black pepper

6 tuna steaks, 6 to 8 oz. each

2 teaspoons parsley, finely chopped

Preheat oven to 350° F.

Serves six – 4.4 carb grams per serving

Heat $^1/_4$ cup of the olive oil in a saucepan and sauté the onion and garlic until soft. Add the olives, vinegar, lemon juice, oregano, salt and pepper; continue to cook, while stirring, for 3 to 4 minutes. Grease a baking dish with the remaining $^1/_4$ cup olive oil and place tuna in dish. Spoon the sauce over the tuna, cover with foil and bake for 20 to 25 minutes. Sprinkle with parsley and serve.

Sweet Pepper and Mushroom Chicken

4 lbs. assorted chicken pieces

1 teaspoon salt

$^1/_2$ teaspoon black pepper

4 tablespoons olive oil

$^1/_2$ cup butter or margarine

1 large onion, finely chopped

1 teaspoon garlic, minced

14 oz. canned tomatoes, drained and chopped

1 cup dry white wine

1 cup chicken broth or stock

1 cup chopped green bell pepper

1 cup chopped red bell pepper

2 cups mushrooms, sliced

$^1/_2$ teaspoon oregano

$^1/_2$ teaspoon thyme

2 tablespoons parsley, finely chopped

salt and pepper to taste

Serves six – 11.3 carb grams per serving

Season the chicken with the salt and pepper. In a large pot, heat 2 tablespoons of the olive oil over medium-high heat and cook the chicken until lightly browned on both sides. Remove the chicken from the pot and dispose of the fat residue. Add the remaining olive oil and the butter or margarine to the same pot and sauté the onion and garlic until soft. Return the chicken to the pot, add the tomatoes, wine, broth or stock, peppers, mushrooms, oregano, thyme and parsley. Bring to a boil, reduce to low heat, cover and simmer for 30 to 40 minutes or until chicken is tender. Salt and pepper to taste before serving.

Raspberry Chicken

5 lbs. assorted chicken pieces

3 cups raspberries

1 cup raspberry vinegar

1 cup olive oil

1 cup green onion, finely chopped

3 bay leaves

$^1/_2$ teaspoon thyme

$^1/_2$ teaspoon basil

1 teaspoon salt

$^1/_2$ teaspoon black pepper

Heat the broiler

Serves six – 12.6 carb grams per serving

In a saucepan, boil for about 1 minute the raspberries and vinegar. Remove from heat and gradually stir in the olive oil, green onion, bay leaves, thyme and basil. Cool the marinade to room temperature; then sprinkle the chicken with salt and pepper. Coat the chicken pieces with the marinade, stirring occasionally and refrigerate overnight. Place the chicken in a broiling pan, baste frequently with the marinade and cook until done.

Creamed Lemon Chicken with Asparagus

$^3/_4$ cup butter or margarine

6 boneless chicken breasts, about 8 oz. each

3 cups asparagus, cut into $^1/_2$ inch pieces

1 small onion, finely chopped

$^1/_2$ cup green onion, finely chopped

1 cup chicken broth or stock

6 tablespoons lemon juice

$1^1/_2$ cups cream

$^1/_2$ cup dry white wine

2 tablespoons fresh parsley, finely chopped

3 teaspoons grated lemon zest

$1^1/_2$ teaspoons salt

$^1/_2$ teaspoon black pepper

Serves six – 9.1 carb grams per serving

In a large skillet, melt the butter or margarine and cook the chicken over medium heat on both sides until golden brown. Remove the chicken from the skillet; then add the asparagus, onions, broth or stock and lemon juice to the skillet. Reduce the heat to medium-low and cook until the asparagus are tender. Return the chicken to the skillet and stir in the cream, wine, parsley, lemon zest, salt and pepper. Bring the mixture to a boil and cook until chicken is done and cream sauce is reduced. Serve and enjoy!

Thai Glazed Chicken

4 garlic cloves, minced

4 tablespoons balsamic vinegar

4 tablespoons soy sauce

4 tablespoons peanut oil

$^1/_2$ teaspoon orange zest

$^1/_4$ teaspoon cayenne pepper

5 lbs. assorted chicken pieces

4 green onions, sliced

Preheat oven to 375° F.

Serves eight – 3.3 carb grams per serving

In a large bowl, combine the garlic, vinegar, soy sauce, peanut oil, zest and cayenne pepper. Toss the chicken pieces in the mixture and marinate at room temperature for 30 minutes, stirring occasionally. Place the chicken pieces in a roasting pan and evenly spread the marinade atop each piece. Bake for 1 hour or until done, basting several times. Serve the chicken on a large platter and garnish with green onion slices.

Peppercorn Chicken

8 boneless chicken breasts, 4 to 6 oz. each

$^1/_2$ cup cracked black peppercorns

Cooking spray

2 cups butter or margarine

1 teaspoon salt

1 tablespoon lemon juice

3 tablespoons parsley, finely chopped

Heat the broiler

Serves eight – 7.2 carb grams per serving

Pound the cracked peppercorns into both sides of the chicken breasts. In a saucepan, melt the butter or margarine; then add the salt, lemon juice and parsley. Spray the broiling pan with cooking spray. Place the chicken breasts on the broiling pan, baste with the butter or margarine mixture and broil for 15 minutes. Turn the chicken breasts over and baste the other side with more of the mixture. Broil for another 15 minutes or until done. Place the chicken on individual plates; mix the remaining butter or margarine mixture with the pan drippings. Top each chicken breast with sauce before serving.

Crustless Chicken Pizza

$^1/_2$ cup butter or margarine

1 large onion, thinly sliced

$2^1/_2$ cups mushrooms, sliced

$^2/_3$ cup dry white wine

4 boneless chicken breasts, 4 to 6 oz. each, pounded

$^1/_2$ teaspoon Italian seasoning

1 teaspoon black pepper

4 thick slices tomato

1 cup shredded Mozzarella cheese

1 tablespoon Dijon mustard

Preheat oven to 350° F.

Serves four – 9.1 carb grams per serving

In a saucepan, heat $^1/_4$ cup of the butter or margarine and sauté the onion and mushrooms until soft. Add the wine and bring to a boil, cooking for about 2 to 3 minutes. Pour the mixture into a bowl and set aside. In the same saucepan, heat the remaining $^1/_4$ cup of butter or margarine. Place the chicken in the saucepan and sprinkle with the Italian seasoning and $^1/_2$ teaspoon of the black pepper. Sauté the chicken until lightly browned; then turn, sprinkle with remaining black pepper and cook until done.

In a baking pan, place the chicken breasts and coat each with 1 teaspoon of the mustard. Top each breast with a slice of tomato, then $^1/_4$ of the onion-mushroom mixture and $^1/_4$ cup of the Mozzarella cheese. Bake in the oven until cheese is melted and serve immediately.

Chicken Cacciatore

$1/4$ cup cooking oil

3 lbs. assorted chicken pieces

1 teaspoon salt

$1/4$ teaspoon black pepper

$1/8$ teaspoon crushed red pepper

1 medium onion, sliced

$1/2$ teaspoon garlic, minced

$1/2$ cup parsley, finely chopped

1 cup dry red wine

28 oz. chopped canned tomatoes

1 cup fresh mushrooms, sliced

1 teaspoon basil

1 teaspoon rosemary

1 teaspoon oregano

salt and pepper to taste

Serves six – 9.86 carb grams per serving

In a large saucepan, heat the cooking oil. Season the chicken with the salt and peppers and place in the saucepan. Cook over medium-high heat, turning each piece until lightly browned on each side. Add the onion, garlic, parsley and sauté until soft. Add the wine, tomatoes, mushrooms, basil, rosemary and oregano. Bring to a boil, then reduce the heat to medium-low. Cover and allow to simmer for 30 to 40 minutes. Salt and pepper to taste before serving.

Chicken Parmigiana

6 boneless chicken breasts, 6 to 8 oz. each

1 teaspoon salt

$^1/_4$ teaspoon black pepper

$^1/_2$ teaspoon oregano

1 cup olive oil

2 cups tomato sauce

$1^1/_2$ cups shredded Mozzarella cheese

1 cup grated Parmesan cheese

Preheat oven to 350° F.

Serves six – 5.5 carb grams per serving

Season the chicken breasts with the salt, pepper and oregano. In a large skillet, heat the olive oil over medium-high heat and cook the chicken breasts until done. Place the chicken breasts in a baking dish and evenly cover the tops with tomato sauce; then sprinkle with both cheeses and bake for 20 minutes or until cheese is browned and melted.

Chicken Piccata

6 boneless chicken breasts, about 6 to 8 oz. each

1 teaspoon salt

$^1/_2$ teaspoon black pepper

$^1/_4$ cup butter or margarine

1 tablespoon olive oil

$^1/_2$ cup dry white wine

1 cup chicken broth or stock

3 tablespoons lemon juice

2 tablespoons capers, drained

2 tablespoons parsley, finely chopped

Serves six – 0.8 carb gram per serving

Season the chicken breasts with the salt and pepper; then melt the butter or margarine with the olive oil in a frying pan. Add the chicken breasts to the frying pan and cook over medium heat until golden brown. Remove the chicken from the pan and set aside. Pour the wine and chicken stock or broth into the pan and bring to a boil; reduce the liquid by $^1/_2$. Add the lemon juice, capers and parsley to the pan; pour over chicken before serving.

Tijuaña Chicken

12 cherry tomatoes, halved

1 avocado, peeled, pitted and finely chopped

3 tablespoons onion, finely chopped

3 fresh basil leaves, shredded

1 tablespoon cilantro, finely chopped

2 tablespoons plus 4 tablespoons olive oil

3 teaspoons lime juice

1 teaspoon garlic, minced

1 teaspoon chili powder

1 teaspoon salt

1 teaspoon black pepper

6 boneless chicken breasts, 6 to 8 oz. each

2 tablespoons parsley, finely chopped

3 limes, quartered for garnish

Heat the broiler

Serves six – 5.4 carb grams per serving

In a medium-sized bowl, combine the tomatoes, avocado, onion, basil, cilantro, 2 tablespoons of the olive oil, lime juice, garlic, $^1/_2$ teaspoon of the chili powder, $^1/_2$ teaspoon of the salt and $^1/_2$ teaspoon of the pepper. Rub the chicken breasts with the remaining olive oil, then season with the remaining chili powder, salt and pepper. Place in a broiling pan and cook until done. Divide the chicken among six individual plates and top with the avocado salsa. Sprinkle with parsley and garnish with limes. Enjoy!

Chicken Chili

$^1/_2$ cup cooking oil

1 cup chopped onion

1 cup chopped green pepper

1 teaspoon garlic, minced

1 tablespoon jalapeno pepper, finely chopped

1 tablespoon oregano

2 teaspoons cumin

1 tablespoon chili powder

$^1/_8$ teaspoon cayenne pepper

2 tablespoons lime juice

4 cups tomato sauce

2 cups chicken broth or stock

1 cup canned diced tomatoes and green chiles, drained

$^1/_2$ teaspoon granulated Sweet 'N Low®

5 cups chopped, boneless chicken breasts

$^1/_2$ cup cilantro, finely chopped

1 cup grated Cheddar cheese

Serves eight – 12.3 carb grams per serving

In a large pot, heat the cooking oil and bring the next 11 ingredients to a boil. Reduce the heat and simmer for about 1 hour. Add the tomatoes, chiles, Sweet 'N Low® and chicken; continue cooking over low heat until chicken is done. Sprinkle with cilantro and Cheddar cheese before serving.

Baja Chicken Wraps

4 boneless chicken breasts, cooked and sliced

$^1/_2$ cup chopped green chiles, drained

1 cup chopped tomato

$^1/_2$ cup green onion, finely chopped

$^1/_2$ cup onion, finely chopped

$^1/_2$ cup shredded Cheddar cheese

$^1/_2$ cup shredded Monterey Jack cheese

8 large lettuce leaves

2 cups shredded iceberg lettuce

1 cup salsa

$^1/_2$ cup sour cream

Serves eight – 5.3 carb grams per serving

In a bowl, combine the chicken slices, chiles, tomato, onions and cheeses. Place each lettuce leaf on individual plates and fill each with an even portion of the chicken mixture. Sprinkle the tops with shredded lettuce; then spoon salsa and sour cream atop each wrap before serving. Roll up like a taco and enjoy!

Julius Caesar's Chicken Wrap

2 garlic cloves, minced

$^2/_3$ cup olive oil

2 tablespoons red wine vinegar

1 tablespoon lemon juice

1 teaspoon Worcestershire sauce

1 teaspoon anchovy paste or chopped anchovies

2 dashes Tabasco®

$^1/_2$ teaspoon black pepper

$^1/_2$ cup plus $^1/_2$ cup grated Parmesan cheese

4 boneless chicken breasts, cooked and sliced

2 cups chopped romaine lettuce

8 large lettuce leaves

Serves eight – 1.7 carb grams per serving

In a blender, combine the first 8 ingredients and $^1/_2$ cup of the Parmesan cheese until smooth. Toss the sliced chicken with the romaine lettuce and the remaining $^1/_2$ cup of Parmesan cheese with the blended dressing. Place each large lettuce leaf on an individual plate and fill with the chicken Caesar mixture. Roll up like a taco and enjoy!

Chicken Créole

¼ cup cooking oil

4 lbs. assorted chicken pieces

1 teaspoon garlic, minced

1 cup chopped onion

1 cup chopped ham

6 bacon strips, cooked crisp and crumbled

2 cups chopped tomato

2 tablespoons parsley, finely chopped

¼ teaspoon Tabasco®

2 teaspoons salt

½ teaspoon black pepper

2 cups boiling water

2 cups okra, cooked and chopped

Serves six – 8.1 carb grams per serving

In a large skillet, heat the cooking oil and brown the chicken pieces on all sides; then remove. Add the garlic and onion; sauté until soft. Stir in the ham, bacon, tomato, parsley, Tabasco,® salt, pepper and water. Return the chicken to the skillet; cover and cook over medium-low heat for 45 to 60 minutes. During the last 10 minutes, add the okra to the mixture before serving.

Spinach Stuffed Chicken Breasts Gratinée

2 tablespoons olive oil

1 cup onion, finely chopped

1 teaspoon garlic, minced

10 oz. frozen spinach, thawed and drained

3 tablespoons parsley, finely chopped

$1/2$ teaspoon basil

$1/2$ teaspoon rosemary

1 cup shredded Swiss cheese

$1/4$ cup grated Parmesan cheese

1 egg

$1/2$ teaspoon salt

$1/2$ teaspoon black pepper

6 boneless chicken breasts, 6 to 8 oz. each

Preheat oven to 375° F.

Serves six – 5.6 carb grams per serving

Heat the olive oil in a large skillet and sauté the onion and garlic until soft. Stir in the spinach, parsley, basil and rosemary; cook for about 3 minutes. Remove the skillet from the heat and allow to cool. Mix the Swiss and Parmesan cheeses, egg, salt and pepper with the spinach mixture in a large bowl. Slit each chicken breast, down the center, creating a pocket. Stuff each pocket with the spinach-cheese mixture. Bake the chicken on a greased baking dish for 45 to 60 minutes or until done.

Creamed Chicken and Broccoli

4 boneless chicken breasts, cooked and chopped

4 cups broccoli, cooked and drained

1 cup butter or margarine

4 cups cream

$1^1/_2$ cups grated Parmesan cheese

1 teaspoon black pepper

Serves four – 12.1 carb grams per serving

In a large saucepan, melt the butter or margarine over medium heat; add the cream and bring to a boil. Reduce to a low-boil and cook for 4 to 5 minutes, until thick. Stir in $^3/_4$ cup of the Parmesan cheese and cook for 2 minutes before removing from heat. Pour the chicken and broccoli into the saucepan; toss with the cheese sauce until well coated. Then sprinkle with the remaining cheese and black pepper; toss well before serving.

Citrus Turkey

$^3/_4$ cup butter or margarine

$^1/_2$ cup lime juice

4 teaspoons dry mustard

1 tablespoon garlic powder

$^1/_2$ teaspoon salt

$^1/_2$ teaspoon black pepper

3 lbs. boneless turkey breast, sliced

Heat the broiler

Serves six – 3.4 carb grams per serving

In a saucepan, over low heat, combine the butter or margarine, lime juice, mustard and garlic powder. Season the turkey slices with the salt and pepper and place in a broiling pan. Pour the marinade over the turkey and cook until done, occasionally basting. Enjoy!

Turkey Wings Cacciatore with Mushrooms

8 turkey wings, tips discarded

1 teaspoon salt

1 teaspoon black pepper

$^1/_2$ cup olive oil

1 cup chopped onion

1 cup chopped green pepper

2 tablespoons parsley, finely chopped

2 garlic cloves, minced

2 cups fresh mushrooms, sliced

2 cups chopped tomato

2 cups tomato sauce

2 cups dry red wine

1 teaspoon oregano

$^1/_2$ cup grated Parmesan cheese

$^1/_2$ teaspoon granulated Sweet 'N Low®

Heat the broiler

Serves eight – 10.5 carb grams per serving

Season the turkey wings with the salt and pepper; broil, turning until evenly browned. In a large pot, heat the olive oil and sauté the onion, green pepper, parsley and garlic until soft. Add all remaining ingredients; cover and simmer over low heat, stirring occasionally until turkey is tender. Uncover and cook another 20 minutes until sauce has thickened before serving.

Sloppiest Turkey Joes

3 tablespoons olive oil

2 lbs. ground turkey

2 cups chopped onion

$^1/_2$ cup chopped celery

1 cup chopped green pepper

4 garlic cloves, minced

$1^1/_2$ cups tomato sauce

$^1/_3$ cup Worcestershire sauce

1 cup water

1 teaspoon salt

1 teaspoon black pepper

4 dashes Tabasco®

$^1/_2$ teaspoon Sweet 'N Low®

6 large lettuce leaves

Serves six – 13.5 carb grams per serving

In a large skillet, heat the olive oil and cook the turkey until brown. Add the onion, celery, green pepper and garlic; cook until soft. Add the remaining ingredients, except for the lettuce leaves, and simmer for 30 to 45 minutes. Spoon the mixture into each lettuce leaf and eat like a taco.

Spicy Turkey Cheeseburgers

2 lbs. ground turkey

1 cup chopped onion

1 cup chopped green pepper

2 teaspoons garlic, minced

1 teaspoon paprika

1 teaspoon crushed red pepper

6 dashes Tabasco®

2 cups grated Cheddar cheese

Heat the broiler

Serves eight – 3.7 carb grams per serving

In a bowl, mix the turkey with all of the ingredients except for the Cheddar cheese. Form the turkey mixture into eight patties. Broil the turkey burgers for about 6 minutes on each side or until done. Top each patty with the Cheddar cheese and allow to melt before serving.

Pork Roast Marsala

4 lb. pork loin roast

1 teaspoon oregano

1 teaspoon thyme

1 teaspoon salt

$^1/_2$ teaspoon black pepper

4 garlic cloves, cut into slivers

2 tablespoons butter or margarine

2 tablespoons olive oil

2 garlic cloves, minced

1 cup marsala

1 cup dry red wine

2 tablespoons tomato paste

1 lb. fresh mushrooms, sliced

2 tablespoons parsley, finely chopped

Preheat oven to 375° F.

Serves six – 10.6 carb grams per serving

Cut small slits into the roast. In a small bowl, mix together the oregano, thyme, salt and pepper. Coat the garlic slivers with the spice mixture. Insert the garlic slivers into the slits in the roast and rub the remaining mixture over the top of the meat. Place the meat in a roasting pan.

In a skillet over medium heat, melt the butter or margarine and olive oil; sauté the minced garlic cloves until soft. Add the wines and tomato paste, blending well. Then add the mushrooms and parsley; simmer for 5 to 6 minutes. Pour the mixture over the roast and cover. Cook for $1^1/_2$ to 2 hours, basting occasionally with the sauce.

Pork Chops with Garlic Cream

¹/2 cup olive oil

6 garlic cloves, minced

8 pork chops, ¹/2 inch thick

2 teaspoons basil

¹/2 teaspoon salt

¹/2 teaspoon black pepper

1 cup cream

Serves six – 2.5 carb grams per serving

In a large skillet, over medium-high heat, sauté the garlic until soft in ¹/4 cup of the olive oil. Add the pork chops and sauté on each side until brown.

In a small bowl, combine the remaining ¹/4 cup olive oil, basil, salt and pepper. Baste the pork chops with the mixture; continue to cook the pork chops until done. Remove the pork chops from the skillet; then whisk the cream with pan drippings over medium heat until the sauce thickens. Pour the sauce over the pork chops before serving.

Lamb Burgers

2 lbs. ground lamb

¹/2 cup chopped onion

¹/2 teaspoon garlic, minced

2 tablespoons parsley, finely chopped

2 teaspoons rosemary, finely chopped

¹/4 teaspoon cumin

¹/2 teaspoon salt

¹/2 teaspoon black pepper

1¹/2 tablespoons Worcestershire sauce

Heat the broiler

Serves four – 3.3 carb grams per serving

In a bowl, combine the lamb with all of the ingredients except for the Worcestershire sauce. Divide the lamb and form into four patties. Place the patties on a broiling pan and broil for 4 to 6 minutes on each side. Blend the Worcestershire sauce with the pan drippings before serving.

Roasted Tenderloin of Lamb

5 lb. lamb tenderloin or roast

1 teaspoon rosemary

$^1/_2$ teaspoon thyme

1 teaspoon salt

$^1/_2$ teaspoon black pepper

5 garlic cloves, cut into slivers

2 tablespoons plus $^1/_2$ cup butter or margarine

2 tablespoons olive oil

2 garlic cloves, minced

2 cups dry red wine

$^1/_2$ cup Worcestershire sauce

2 tablespoons parsley, finely chopped

Preheat oven to 375° F.

Serves six – 6.4 carb grams per serving

Cut small slits into the lamb. In a small bowl, mix together the rosemary, thyme, salt and pepper. Coat the garlic slivers with the spice mixture. Insert the garlic slivers into the slits in the lamb and rub the remaining mixture over the top of the meat. Place the meat in a roasting pan.

In a skillet over medium heat, melt the 2 tablespoons butter or margarine and olive oil; sauté the minced garlic cloves until soft. Add the wine, blending well. Then add the Worcestershire sauce, $^1/_2$ cup butter or margarine and parsley; simmer for 5 to 6 minutes. Pour the mixture over the lamb and cover. Cook for $1^1/_2$ to 2 hours, basting occasionally with the sauce.

Freshly Minted Lamb Chops

8 lamb chops, 6 to 8 oz. each

$1/4$ cup olive oil

3 tablespoons Dijon mustard

2 tablespoons lemon juice

2 tablespoons Worcestershire sauce

1 tablespoon garlic, minced

1 cup fresh mint leaves, minced

$1/2$ cup parsley, minced

$1/2$ teaspoon salt

$1/2$ teaspoon black pepper

Heat the broiler

Serves four – 5.2 carb grams per serving

In a bowl, combine all of the ingredients and coat the lamb chops well with the marinade. Refrigerate for at least 6 hours, turning the chops occasionally. Place the chops on a broiling pan and broil for 6 to 8 minutes on each side for medium doneness; baste occasionally.

Marinated Lamb Wraps

3 lbs. lamb, cooked and sliced

$^1/_2$ cup lemon juice

$^1/_2$ cup balsamic vinegar

$1^1/_2$ cups olive oil

1 teaspoon salt

1 teaspoon black pepper

4 cups chopped tomato

2 cucumbers, peeled and chopped

1 cup chopped green pepper

1 cup chopped green onion

1 cup chopped onion

6 garlic cloves, minced

1 cup fresh mint leaves, minced

$^1/_2$ cup parsley, finely chopped

10 large lettuce leaves

Serves ten – 13.4 carb grams per serving

In a large bowl, whisk together the lemon juice, vinegar, oil, salt and pepper. Add the remaining ingredients, mixing well; refrigerate for at least 6 hours, stirring occasionally. Spoon the mixture evenly into each of the lettuce leaves before serving and eat like a taco.

Veal Stew with Artichokes and Mushrooms

3 lbs. boneless veal, cut into 2 inch pieces

4 tablespoons olive oil

24 pearl onions, peeled

6 garlic cloves

$^1/_2$ cup dry white wine

$1^1/_2$ cups beef broth or stock

$1^1/_2$ cups chicken broth or stock

2 cups fresh mushrooms, sliced

2 cups artichoke hearts, sliced

2 tablespoons parsley, finely chopped

1 teaspoon salt

$^1/_2$ teaspoon black pepper

Serves six – 9.0 carb grams per serving

In a large skillet, heat the olive oil and brown the meat on all sides; set the meat aside. Add the onions and garlic; sauté until soft. Over medium-high heat, add the wine and broths or stocks; blend well, bringing to a boil. Reduce the heat to a low boil, adding the mushrooms, artichokes, parsley, salt and pepper. Return the veal to the pot, cover and simmer for $1^1/_2$ to 2 hours or until meat is very tender.

Veal Roast

5 lb. veal roast

1 tablespoon rosemary

1 teaspoon salt

$^1/_2$ teaspoon black pepper

5 garlic cloves, cut into slivers

2 tablespoons plus $^1/_2$ cup butter or margarine

2 tablespoons olive oil

2 garlic cloves, minced

2 cups dry white wine

$^1/_2$ cup Worcestershire sauce

2 tablespoons parsley, finely chopped

Preheat oven to 375° F.

Serves six – 6.1 carb grams per serving

Cut small slits into the roast. In a small bowl, mix together the rosemary, salt and pepper. Coat the garlic slivers with the spice mixture. Insert the garlic slivers into the slits in the roast and rub the remaining mixture over the top of the meat. Place the meat in a roasting pan.

In a skillet over medium heat, melt the 2 tablespoons butter or margarine and olive oil; sauté the minced garlic cloves until soft. Add the wine, blending well. Then add the Worcestershire sauce, $^1/_2$ cup butter or margarine and parsley; simmer for 5 to 6 minutes. Pour the mixture over the roast and cover. Cook for $1^1/_2$ to 2 hours, basting occasionally with the sauce.

Stuffed Veal Chops

4 veal chops, about 12 to 16 oz. each

4 tablespoons olive oil

$^1/_2$ cup onion, finely chopped

$^1/_4$ cup green pepper, finely chopped

8 garlic cloves, minced

1 tablespoon parsley, finely chopped

$^1/_4$ cup chopped ham

$1^1/_2$ cups chopped spinach

1 tablespoon tarragon

$^1/_2$ teaspoon salt

$^1/_2$ teaspoon black pepper

4 tablespoons crumbled Blue cheese

Preheat oven to 375° F.

Serves four – 5.9 carb grams per serving

Slit a pocket inside each chop. In a large skillet, heat 2 of the tablespoons of olive oil over medium-high heat and brown the chops on both sides. In a medium-sized skillet, heat the remaining olive oil and sauté the onion, pepper, garlic and parsley until soft. Add the ham and spinach, seasoning with tarragon, salt and pepper; sauté for about 2 minutes. Stir in the Blue cheese and stuff each chop with the mixture; then fasten with a toothpick. Place chops in a baking dish and cook until done, about 30 to 40 minutes.

Veal Medallions in Red Wine Sauce

4 medallions of veal, 6 to 8 oz. each

1 teaspoon salt

$^{1}/_{2}$ teaspoon black pepper

1 cup dry red wine

$^{1}/_{2}$ cup butter or margarine

1 cup beef broth or stock

1 tablespoon lemon juice

1 teaspoon dried oregano

$1^{1}/_{2}$ cups fresh mushrooms, sliced

2 cups canned chopped tomatoes

3 tablespoons parsley, finely chopped

Serves four – 8.3 carb grams per serving

Salt and pepper the veal medallions and place in a shallow bowl. Pour the wine over the medallions, cover and marinate in the refrigerator for $1^{1}/_{2}$ to 2 hours. Remove veal from the bowl, reserving the wine. In a large skillet over medium-high heat, melt the butter or margarine and brown the veal on both sides. Add the broth or stock, lemon juice, reserved wine, oregano, mushrooms, tomatoes and parsley; bring to a low boil. Reduce the heat and simmer for about 20 minutes or until done; stir occasionally.

Roquefort-Walnut Hamburgers

4 lbs. ground beef

$1/2$ cup green onion, finely chopped

$1/2$ cup onion, finely chopped

$1/2$ cup green pepper, finely chopped

1 tablespoon garlic, minced

1 teaspoon basil

1 teaspoon oregano

1 teaspoon chili powder

1 teaspoon salt

$1/2$ teaspoon black pepper

4 tablespoons walnut pieces

2 cups crumbled Roquefort cheese

Heat the broiler

Serves eight – 4.0 carb grams per serving

In a bowl, except for the cheese, combine all ingredients. Shape mixture into eight thick hamburger patties. Make a pocket in the center of each patty. Fill each center with the cheese, sprinkling some on top. Place the patties in a broiling pan and cook for 15 minutes; then cook until desired doneness.

Hamburger Brennan

2 lbs. ground beef

$^1/_2$ cup green onion, finely chopped

$^1/_4$ cup onion, finely chopped

2 tablespoons Worcestershire sauce

1 tablespoon chopped fresh parsley

2 large eggs

Pinch of nutmeg

$1^1/_2$ teaspoons salt

1 teaspoon black pepper

$1^1/_2$ cups Sauce Maison (below)

Heat the broiler

Serves six – 3.8 carb grams per serving

Combine all of the ingredients in a large bowl. When the mixture is well combined, shape into 6 oval patties. Place the patties on a broiling pan and broil until your desired doneness; reserve 1 cup cooking juices for preparation of the sauce. Drizzle Sauce Maison on each patty and serve.

Sauce Maison:

$^3/_4$ cup butter or margarine

2 tablespoons Worcestershire sauce

1 cup meat juices (beef broth or stock can be substituted)

1 teaspoon chopped fresh parsley

Yields $1^1/_2$ cups

In a small skillet, cook the butter or margarine over medium heat until golden brown. Stir in the Worcestershire sauce and meat juices (broth or stock); cook for 1 minute. Add the parsley and keep the sauce warm until serving.

175

Beef Chili

1/2 cup cooking oil

4 green peppers, cut into 1 inch pieces

4 medium onions, cut into 1 inch pieces

6 teaspoons garlic, minced

6 lbs. ground beef

2 teaspoons garlic powder

2 tablespoons chili powder

1 1/2 teaspoons granulated Sweet 'N Low®

2 29 oz. cans tomato sauce

2 tablespoons salt

1 tablespoon black pepper

Serves twelve – 15.8 carb grams per serving

In a large pot, sauté the pepper, onion and garlic in the cooking oil over medium heat until soft. Add the beef and brown. Then add the remaining ingredients and cook on medium-low heat for 1 hour. Serve and enjoy!

Beef and Mushroom Fricassee

3 lbs. boneless beef, cut into pieces

$^1/_4$ cup plus $^1/_4$ cup butter or margarine

2 cups chopped onion

2 cups chopped green pepper

1 cup chopped celery

3 garlic cloves, minced

2 tablespoons chopped parsley

4 cups beef broth or stock

$1^1/_2$ cups dry red wine

1 cup water

2 teaspoons salt

1 teaspoon black pepper

$1^1/_2$ cups fresh mushrooms, sliced

Preheat oven to 325° F.

Serves six – 11.5 carb grams per serving

In a large skillet, heat $^1/_4$ cup of the butter or margarine and brown the beef over medium-high heat; place the beef in a bowl and set aside. Melt the remaining $^1/_4$ cup of butter or margarine and blend well with the beef drippings. Add the onion, green pepper, celery, garlic and parsley; sauté until tender. Return the beef to the skillet and add the remaining ingredients. Cover and simmer over medium heat until done.

Garlic Pot Roast of Beef

4 lb. beef roast

1 teaspoon onion powder

1 teaspoon salt

$^1/_2$ teaspoon black pepper

5 garlic cloves, cut into slivers

$^1/_2$ cup cooking oil

2 tablespoons plus $^1/_2$ cup butter or margarine

2 tablespoons olive oil

2 garlic cloves, minced

2 cups dry red wine

$^1/_2$ cup Worcestershire sauce

2 tablespoons parsley, finely chopped

Preheat oven to 375° F.

Serves six – 6.5 carb grams per serving

Cut small slits into the roast. In a small bowl, mix together the onion powder, salt and pepper. Coat the garlic slivers with the spice mixture. Insert the garlic slivers into the slits in the roast and rub the remaining mixture over the top of the meat. Heat the cooking oil in a heavy pot or Dutch oven; add the roast and brown thoroughly on all sides.

In a skillet over medium heat, melt the 2 tablespoons butter or margarine and olive oil; sauté the minced garlic cloves until soft. Add the wine, blending well. Then add the Worcestershire sauce, $^1/_2$ cup butter or margarine and parsley; simmer for 5 to 6 minutes. Pour the mixture over the roast and cover. Cook over low heat for 3 to 4 hours or until meat is tender.

Bridget's Steak Fajitas

¹/₂ cup lime juice

4 tablespoons olive oil

2 tablespoons garlic, minced

2 teaspoons salt

2 teaspoons chili powder

2 lbs. sirloin, thinly sliced

4 tablespoons cooking oil

4 large onions, sliced

2 large green bell peppers, sliced

2 large red bell peppers, sliced

2 cups fresh guacamole

1 cup shredded Cheddar cheese

2 cups salsa

2 cups sour cream

Serves eight – 10.0 carb grams per serving

In a bowl, combine the sliced sirloin the lime juice, olive oil, garlic, salt and chili powder; marinate for 1 hour. Heat the cooking oil in a skillet on high heat; add the steak slices and marinade. Sauté for 2 to 3 minutes then add the onion and peppers. Cook until the meat is done and the vegetables are crispy-tender. Serve steak fajitas topped with guacamole, Cheddar cheese, salsa and sour cream.

Dijon Marinated Beef

2 lb. flank steak

1 cup red wine

$^1/_2$ cup soy sauce

1 tablespoon lemon juice

$^1/_3$ cup vegetable oil

1 teaspoon garlic powder

$^1/_2$ teaspoon onion powder

$^1/_2$ teaspoon oregano

1 teaspoon salt

1 teaspoon black pepper

Heat the broiler

Serves six – 0 carb grams per serving

Place the steak in a broiling pan. In a bowl, combine all the remaining ingredients and pour over the steak. Cover and refrigerate for 6 to 8 hours, turning the steak occasionally; then broil for about $1^1/_2$ hours or until desired doneness.

Smothered Steaks

4 12 oz. sirloin steaks

2 teaspoons ground black pepper

1 teaspoon salt

4 tablespoons butter or margarine

2 cups onion, sliced

$^1/_2$ cup beef broth or stock

$^1/_2$ cup dry red wine

Serves four – 6.2 carb grams per serving

Press pepper onto both sides of sirloins and season with the salt. In a large skillet, over medium heat, melt the butter or margarine and cook the steaks to desired doneness. Transfer the steaks to a serving platter, reserving the drippings in the skillet while keeping the steaks warm. Stir the onion into the drippings and sauté until the onion is tender. Add the broth or stock and wine to the onion mixture, stirring thoroughly. Bring to a boil; then reduce the heat. Cook at a low boil, uncovered, for about 3 minutes until mixture is reduced to preferred consistency. Spoon over steaks and serve.

Steak Diane

4 beef filets, each sliced into 2 medallions

4 tablespoons butter or margarine

3 cloves garlic, minced

1 small white onion, finely chopped

2 stalks celery, finely chopped

3 sprigs parsley, finely chopped

$1^{1}/_{2}$ teaspoons salt

$^{3}/_{4}$ teaspoon black pepper

$^{3}/_{4}$ cup Worcestershire sauce

juice of $^{1}/_{2}$ lemon

3 dashes Tabasco®

Serves four – 13.4 carb grams per serving

Melt the butter or margarine in a large skillet over low heat. Place the slices of meat in the skillet and simmer, on both sides, until medium done. Remove the meat; place on a large serving platter and set aside. Add the garlic, onion, celery, parsley, salt and pepper to the skillet. Simmer for a few minutes then add the Worcestershire sauce, lemon juice and Tabasco.® Cook a little longer until the sauce is slightly thickened. Return the meat to the skillet and cook for about 30 seconds on each side. Then, return the meat to the serving platter and pour the sauce from the skillet on top.

Filet Royale

2 tablespoons butter or margarine

$^1/_2$ cup fresh mushrooms, sliced

$^1/_4$ cup red wine

$^1/_2$ cup beef broth or stock

$^1/_4$ teaspoon Worcestershire sauce

4 filets mignon, 9 oz. each

$^1/_2$ teaspoon plus $^1/_2$ teaspoon salt

$^1/_4$ teaspoon plus $^1/_4$ teaspoon black pepper

Heat the broiler

Serves four – 1.0 carb grams per serving

In a small saucepan, melt the butter or margarine and cook the mushrooms over low heat until tender. Stir in the wine, broth or stock and Worcestershire sauce. Season the sauce with $^1/_2$ teaspoon of the salt and $^1/_4$ teaspoon of the pepper; simmer until slightly reduced. Sprinkle the steaks with the remaining salt and pepper on both sides; then place in a broiling pan and cook until preferred doneness. Place the filets on individual plates and spoon the mushroom sauce on top before serving.

Side Dishes or Vegetarian's Fare

Dijon Asparagus

$^1/_2$ cup sour cream

$1^1/_2$ tablespoons Dijon mustard

2 teaspoons butter or margarine

1 teaspoon fresh parsley, finely chopped

$^1/_4$ teaspoon salt

24 asparagus spears, cooked

Serves four – 6.1 carb grams per serving

In a small saucepan, combine all the ingredients except for the asparagus. Cook over low heat until warm, stirring occasionally. Arrange the asparagus on individual plates and top with the sauce; serve immediately.

Lemon-Dilled Asparagus and Zucchini

1 lb. asparagus, cut into 1 inch pieces

2 large zucchini, cut into strips

3 tablespoons butter or margarine

3 tablespoons lemon juice

1 tablespoon chopped fresh dill

$^1/_2$ teaspoon salt

Serves six – 6.3 carb grams per serving

Steam the asparagus and zucchini until the vegetables are crispy and tender, for about 8 to 10 minutes. Melt the butter or margarine in a saucepan and add the remaining ingredients; blend well. Stir in the asparagus and zucchini, coating thoroughly with the lemon-dill sauce before serving.

Asparagus and Broccoli Au Gratin

2 cups grated Cheddar cheese

2 lbs. fresh asparagus, cooked and cut into 1 inch pieces

2 cups broccoli, cooked and cut into florets

$^1/_3$ cup sour cream

$^2/_3$ cup cream

$^1/_4$ teaspoon salt

$^1/_4$ teaspoon cayenne pepper

Preheat oven to 350° F.

Serves eight – 7.2 carb grams per serving

In a medium-sized bowl, combine 1 cup of the Cheddar cheese and the remaining ingredients. Coat a baking dish with cooking spray and pour in the mixture. Bake for 10 to 15 minutes then sprinkle the remaining Cheddar cheese on top and bake an additional 5 minutes or until golden brown.

Broccoli Parmesan

2 cups broccoli, cooked and chopped

3 tablespoons olive oil

$^1/_2$ cup grated Parmesan cheese

$^1/_2$ tcaspoon basil

$^1/_4$ teaspoon salt

$^1/_4$ teaspoon black pepper

Serves four – 2.5 carb grams per serving

In a saucepan, heat the olive oil and sauté the broccoli for 3 to 4 minutes. Add the remaining ingredients and combine thoroughly before serving.

185

Brussels Sprouts

1/4 cup olive oil

1/2 cup chopped onion

1 tablespoon parsley, finely chopped

1 teaspoon garlic, minced

1/2 teaspoon salt

1/4 teaspoon black pepper

1/2 cup chicken broth or stock

3 cups brussels sprouts, cooked and drained

Serves four – 8.1 carb grams per serving

In a large skillet, heat the oil and sauté the onion, parsley, garlic, salt and pepper until golden. Add the broth or stock and cook for 4 to 6 minutes or until the liquid reduces. Add the brussels sprouts; simmer and serve.

Stewed Cabbage

1 medium head cabbage

1/2 cup water

1/4 teaspoon salt

1/4 teaspoon black pepper

1/2 medium onion, thinly sliced

1 cup diced ham or other seasoning meat

1 tablespoon olive oil, butter or margarine

1/4 teaspoon crushed red pepper

1/2 teaspoon garlic powder

Serves six – 9.6 carb grams per serving

In a large pot or skillet, over medium heat, combine the cabbage with the water, salt and pepper; cover and cook until soft. Uncover and stir in the onion and ham or seasoning meat. Raise to medium-high heat; add the oil, butter or margarine, red pepper and garlic powder. Sauté until onion is soft and cabbage is brown; the water should evaporate before serving.

Oriental Cabbage

$1/2$ cup butter or margarine

1 cup chopped onion

1 cup chopped celery

$1/2$ cup chopped green pepper

1 teaspoon garlic, minced

3 tablespoons soy sauce

$1/2$ teaspoon salt

$1/2$ teaspoon black pepper

4 cups chopped cabbage

Serves six – 8.0 carb grams per serving

In a skillet, melt the butter or margarine and add the remaining ingredients except for the cabbage; sauté until soft. Add the cabbage and simmer until tender before serving.

Mexican Cauliflower

1 large cauliflower, cooked and cut into florets

1 cup chopped tomato

$1/4$ cup butter or margarine, melted

2 tablespoons chopped onion

2 tablespoons chopped green pepper

2 tablespoons chopped parsley

$1/2$ teaspoon chili powder

$1/4$ teaspoon salt

$1/8$ teaspoon cayenne pepper

1 cup grated Cheddar cheese

Preheat oven to 400° F.

Serves four – 4.4 carb grams per serving

In a large bowl, thoroughly combine all of the ingredients except for the Cheddar cheese. Pour the mixture into a lightly greased casserole dish and top with the cheese. Bake for about 30 minutes or until cheese is golden brown.

Spicy Eggplant Casserole

2 large eggplant, cooked and chopped

4 tablespoons butter or margarine

$^1/_2$ cup chopped onion

$^1/_4$ cup chopped green pepper

2 garlic cloves, minced

2 tablespoons chopped parsley

2 jalapeno peppers, minced

$^1/_2$ cup chicken broth or stock

$^1/_2$ cup dry red wine

16 oz. canned chopped tomatoes

$^1/_2$ teaspoon oregano

$^1/_2$ teaspoon salt

$^1/_2$ teaspoon black pepper

4 tablespoons grated Parmesan cheese

Preheat oven to 350° F.

Serves eight – 13.8 carb grams per serving

Melt the butter or margarine in a frying pan and sauté the onion, green pepper, garlic, parsley and jalapeno peppers until soft. Add the eggplant and cook for 10 to 12 minutes, stirring occasionally. In a small saucepan, add the remaining ingredients except for the Parmesan cheese and simmer for 10 minutes; then spoon some of the sauce into a greased casserole dish. Place a layer of the eggplant mixture on top and follow with another layer of the sauce. Continue to alternate until finished. Sprinkle the top with the Parmesan cheese; cover and bake for 30 minutes. Remove the lid and bake until the cheese is lightly brown.

Green Beans Italian Style

2 cups green beans, cooked and chopped

2 tablespoons olive oil

$^1/_2$ cup onion, finely chopped

$^1/_2$ teaspoon garlic, minced

1 tablespoon fresh basil, finely chopped

1 tablespoon fresh parsley, finely chopped

$^1/_2$ teaspoon salt

$^1/_4$ teaspoon black pepper

14 oz. canned tomatoes, drained and chopped

2 tablespoons grated Parmesan cheese

Serves six – 6.5 carb grams per serving

In a skillet, heat the olive oil and sauté the onion, garlic, basil, parsley, salt and pepper over medium heat until soft. Add the tomatoes and cook for about 3 to 5 minutes. Stir in the green beans and cook until well heated. Serve with a sprinkling of Parmesan cheese.

Green Bean and Onion Szechwan

$^1/_2$ cup butter or margarine

2 cups green onion, finely chopped

1 teaspoon parsley, finely chopped

$^1/_2$ teaspoon ginger, finely chopped

1 tablespoon soy sauce

2 tablespoons chopped peanuts

2 teaspoons crushed red pepper

$^1/_4$ teaspoon salt

2 cups green beans, cooked and cut into 1 inch pieces

1 cup mushrooms, sliced, cooked and drained

Serves six – 6.6 carb grams per serving

In a large skillet, melt the butter or margarine and sauté the onion, parsley and ginger until soft. Add the soy sauce, peanuts, pepper and salt; allow to simmer for 3 to 4 minutes. Add the green beans and mushrooms to the skillet; coat well with the mixture. Simmer for 10 to 12 minutes before serving.

189

Stewed Okra Evangeline

1/2 cup cooking oil

4 cups okra, cut into 1/2 inch slices

2 cups chopped ham

1 cup onion, finely chopped

1/2 cup celery, finely chopped

1/2 cup green pepper, finely chopped

2 teaspoons garlic, minced

2 tablespoons parsley, finely chopped

16 oz. canned tomato sauce

1/4 cup water

4 bay leaves

3/4 teaspoon salt

1/8 teaspoon cayenne pepper

1/4 teaspoon black pepper

Serves eight – 9.5 carb grams per serving

In a large skillet, heat the oil and sauté the next 7 ingredients until soft; stir occasionally. Gradually stir in the tomato sauce, water and remaining seasonings. Cover and cook over very low heat, stirring frequently, until the okra is tender to taste.

Tomato and Bacon Spaghetti Squash

1 large summer squash

1 cup chopped tomato

1/2 cup bacon, cooked crisp and crumbled

1/2 teaspoon garlic powder

1/4 teaspoon salt

1/4 teaspoon black pepper

1/4 cup olive oil, butter or margarine, melted

1/2 cup grated Parmesan cheese

Preheat oven to 350° F.

Serves four – 6.0 carb grams per serving

Cut the squash lengthwise and remove seeds. Place the squash, cut-side down, on a baking dish and cook for 45 minutes, turning until tender. When the squash is done, scrape the squash with a fork, pulling out strands of the vegetable. Thoroughly toss the spaghetti squash with the remaining ingredients and serve.

Squash and Zucchini Gratinée

$^1/_4$ cup olive oil

$^1/_2$ cup chopped onion

$^1/_2$ cup chopped green pepper

1 teaspoon garlic, minced

2 eggs

2 tablespoons butter or margarine, melted

$^1/_2$ teaspoon salt

$^1/_4$ teaspoon black pepper

$^1/_8$ teaspoon cayenne pepper

2 cups squash, cooked and chopped

2 cups zucchini, cooked and chopped

1 cup plus $^1/_2$ cup grated Cheddar cheese

Preheat oven to 350º F.

Serves eight – 4.2 carb grams per serving

In a small skillet, heat the olive oil and sauté the onion, green pepper and garlic until soft. In a large bowl, beat the eggs and blend with the butter or margarine, salt and peppers. Add the squash, zucchini, sautéed mixture and 1 cup of the Cheddar cheese, mixing well. Pour into a greased casserole dish, sprinkle with the remaining $^1/_2$ cup cheese and bake, uncovered, until golden.

Shanghai Spinach

$^1/_4$ cup olive oil

1 teaspoon garlic, minced

$^1/_2$ cup scallions, thinly sliced

2 cups spinach, cooked and chopped

1 tablespoon soy sauce

$^1/_4$ teaspoon dried ginger

$^1/_2$ teaspoon black pepper

Serves four – 2.3 carb grams per serving

In a saucepan, over medium heat, sauté the garlic and scallions in the olive oil until soft. Toss the spinach into the mixture and cook until well heated. Season with the soy sauce, ginger and black pepper, mixing well, before serving.

Creamed Spinach

2 tablespoons butter or margarine

2 cups spinach, cooked and chopped

1$^{1}/_{2}$ cups sour cream

1 teaspoon onion powder

1 teaspoon salt

1 teaspoon black pepper

Serves four – 5.0 carb grams per serving

In a saucepan, over medium heat, melt the butter or margarine; stir in the spinach and heat well. In a bowl, combine the remaining ingredients. Add the mixture to the saucepan and cook the spinach mixture for about 3 to 5 minutes before serving.

Grilled Tomatoes

2 large ripe tomatoes

$^{1}/_{2}$ cup grated Parmesan cheese

Preheat oven to 375° F.

Serves four – 4.7 carb grams per serving

Slice each tomato in half, crosswise. Bake on a greased baking sheet until soft. Sprinkle the tomatoes with Parmesan cheese and broil until the cheese melts.

Stuffed Tomatoes

8 medium-sized tomatoes

$1/2$ cup butter or margarine

2 cups mushrooms, sliced

1 cup sour cream

$1/2$ cup crumbled Stilton cheese, room temperature

$1/4$ teaspoon salt

$1/2$ teaspoon black pepper

2 tablespoons chopped almonds

1 tablespoon parsley, finely chopped

Paprika for garnish

Preheat oven to 375° F.

Serves eight – 8.4 carb grams per serving

Slice off the tops of the tomatoes and spoon out the soft insides. Turn the tomatoes upside-down to drain. In a saucepan, over medium heat, melt the butter and sauté the mushrooms until crispy-tender. Stir in the sour cream and cook over low heat until bubbly. Add the cheese, salt and pepper; stir until smooth and then allow to cool. Stuff the tomatoes with the mixture; top with the almonds, parsley and paprika. Bake for about 20 minutes before serving.

Sautéed Zucchini

3 tablespoons olive oil

6 cups zucchini, sliced

$1/2$ cup butter or margarine

2 teaspoons fresh mint, finely chopped

2 teaspoons garlic, minced

$1/2$ teaspoon dry mustard

1 teaspoon salt

$1/2$ teaspoon black pepper

Serves six – 4.3 carb grams per serving

In a large skillet, over medium heat, sauté the zucchini in the olive oil until crispy-tender; drain and set aside. In the same skillet, melt the butter or margarine and thoroughly blend the remaining ingredients. Return the zucchini to the skillet; combine well with the butter or margarine sauce and heat before serving.

Zucchini Stew

½ cup olive oil

1 cup chopped onion

2 teaspoons garlic, minced

3 cups zucchini, cut into 2 inch pieces

1 cup green bell pepper, cut into 1 inch pieces

1 cup red bell pepper, cut into 1 inch pieces

2 cups chopped tomato

1 cup tomato sauce

2 tablespoons chopped parsley

1 teaspoon oregano

½ teaspoon rosemary

¼ teaspoon basil

¼ teaspoon thyme

1 cup water

1 teaspoon salt

½ teaspoon black pepper

Serves eight – 9.7 carb grams per serving

In a large pan, over medium heat, sauté the onion and garlic in the olive oil until soft. Add the zucchini and peppers; cook until tender-crisp. Add the remaining ingredients and bring to a boil. Reduce the heat to low; cover and cook until vegetables are done. Uncover and increase the heat to medium-high; cook until sauce has reduced.

Desserts and Dessert Beverages

Heavenly Chocolate Pie

Meringue Crust (see Index)

1³/₄ oz. chocolate (60-70% cocoa content)

1 pint plus 2 cups whipping cream

1 teaspoon liquid Sweet 'N Low®

3 egg whites

1 teaspoon vanilla extract

¹/₂ teaspoon granulated Sweet 'N Low®

¹/₄ cup chopped nuts (optional)

Serves eight – 7.8 carb grams per serving

Prepare the Meringue Crust and set aside. In a double boiler, melt the chocolate; then in a separate bowl beat 1 pint of the whipping cream until stiff, gradually adding the liquid Sweet 'N Low.® In another bowl, whip the egg whites until stiff peaks form. Mix ¹/₂ of the whipped cream into the melted chocolate, blending well; then mix in the remaining whipped cream. Gradually, fold in the egg whites, thoroughly combining with the chocolate mixture. Spread the chocolate filling evenly over the Meringue Crust and refrigerate for at least 2 hours. Before serving, whip the remaining 2 cups of whipping cream with the vanilla extract and granulated Sweet 'N Low® until stiff peaks form. Gently, spread evenly on top of pie and sprinkle with nuts if desired.

Meringue Crust

3 egg whites

4 teaspoons granulated Sweet 'N Low®

¹/₄ teaspoon baking soda

¹/₈ teaspoon cream tartar

1 teaspoon vanilla extract

Preheat oven to 350° F.

Serves eight – 1.7 carb grams per serving

Beat all ingredients until stiff peaks form. Place in a greased 9 inch pie pan and bake for 20 minutes. Pie crust will rise while baking, but will fall once cooled.

Créole Cream Cheese Pie

Pecan Crust (see Index)

3 eggs, separated

$1/4$ cup plus $3/4$ cup cold water

1 tablespoon unflavored gelatin

5 tablespoons granulated Sweet 'N Low®

16 oz. cream cheese, room temperature

1 cup heavy cream

$1/4$ cup lemon juice

$1/8$ teaspoon salt

Serves eight – 11.5 carb grams per serving

Prepare Pecan Crust and set aside. Pour gelatin into $1/4$ cup of cold water and also set aside. In a large saucepan, combine the egg yolks, remaining $3/4$ cup of water and Sweet 'N Low.® Over medium heat, cook the mixture for about 10 minutes; stir frequently. Stir in gelatin/water then set aside.

In a large bowl, using an electric mixer, thoroughly combine the cream cheese, lemon juice and egg yolk mixture.

In a chilled bowl, whip the heavy cream until soft peaks form. Then, gradually add the egg whites and salt to the cream cheese mixture; blend well. Fold the whipped cream into the cream cheese mixture until well combined.

Pour blended mixture atop Pecan Crust in 9 x 3-inch spring-form pan. Refrigerate overnight before serving.

Pecan Crust

1¹/₄ cups pecans, finely chopped

1¹/₂ teaspoons granulated Sweet 'N Low®

¹/₄ cup butter or margarine, melted

Preheat oven to 350° F.

Serves eight – 3.1 carb grams per serving

In a large bowl, thoroughly combine all of the ingredients. Remove the sides of a 9 x 3-inch spring-form pan, and manually spread the mixture over the bottom of the pan. Bake for 5 to 10 minutes. Remove from oven and reattach the bottom of the pan with the sides of the pan; allow to cool.

Baked Vanilla Custard

3 eggs, beaten

2 tablespoons granulated Sweet 'N Low®

¹/₄ teaspoon salt

2 cups cream, warmed

1¹/₄ teaspoons vanilla extract

Preheat oven to 350° F.

Serves six – 5.6 carb grams per serving

In a large bowl, thoroughly blend the eggs, Sweet 'N Low® and salt. Then, gradually, add the cream and vanilla extract. In a baking dish, at least 2 inches deep, place 6 custard cups. Pour the custard mixture evenly among the custard cups and fill the baking dish with hot water, about 1 inch high. Bake for 1 to 1¹/₂ hours; then chill in the refrigerator for at least 2 hours before serving.

Strawberry Flan Fitzgerald

3 tablespoons plus 1 tablespoon butter or margarine, softened

$^1/_4$ teaspoon salt

2 cups heavy cream

1 teaspoon vanilla extract

2 teaspoons plus 2 teaspoons granulated Sweet 'N Low®

4 egg whites

6 egg yolks

1 pint fresh strawberries, washed and chopped

1 teaspoon strawberry extract

juice of $^1/_2$ lemon

Preheat oven to 350° F.

Serves eight – 6.5 carb grams per serving

In a large bowl, thoroughly blend 3 tablespoons of the butter or margarine with the salt, cream, vanilla extract and 2 teaspoons of the granulated Sweet 'N Low.® In a separate bowl, beat the egg whites until stiff. Add egg yolks to the cream mixture and gradually fold in the egg whites. Pour mixture into a greased 9 inch square baking dish and bake for 45 to 50 minutes.

While flan is baking, melt the remaining 1 tablespoon of butter or margarine in a large skillet. Add the strawberries, strawberry extract, lemon juice and remaining 2 teaspoons Sweet 'N Low.® Cook for about 5 minutes over medium-high heat; then set aside.

When flan is done, remove from the oven and allow to cool. Top each serving with the strawberry mixture and enjoy!

Lemon Pudding

8 egg yolks

1 cup butter or margarine, room temperature

$3^{1}/_{2}$ teaspoons granulated Sweet 'N Low®

6 tablespoons lemon juice

3 teaspoons grated lemon zest

Serves six – 3.6 carb grams per serving

In a medium-sized bowl, beat the egg yolks; then thoroughly blend in the butter or margarine. Pour the mixture into a double boiler and cook over medium-high heat, stirring constantly, until the mixture begins to coat the sides of the pot or the back of the spoon. Remove from the stove and add Sweet 'N Low,® lemon juice and lemon zest; beat until creamy. Pour the pudding mixture into individual cups and allow to chill for at least 2 hours before serving.

Mocha Pudding

$^{1}/_{2}$ oz. unsweetened chocolate, finely chopped

1 cup hot coffee

1 cup heavy cream

5 teaspoons granulated Sweet 'N Low®

$^{1}/_{8}$ teaspoon salt

2 eggs

Serves six – 4.6 carb grams per serving

In a blender, combine all of the ingredients. In a baking dish, at least 2 inches deep, place 6 pudding cups. Pour the pudding mixture evenly among the pudding cups and fill the baking dish with hot water, about 1 inch high. Bake for 1 hour; then allow to cool before serving. May also be served chilled.

Chocolate Mousse

2 cups heavy whipping cream

8 oz. chocolate (60-70% cocoa content), finely chopped

1 teaspoon vanilla extract

$1/4$ teaspoon almond extract

$1^1/2$ teaspoons liquid Sweet 'N Low®

Serves six – 14.3 carb grams per serving

Pour 1 cup heavy cream into a saucepan, bring just to a boil and remove from heat. Whisk in chocolate until smooth; add extracts. Beat remaining 1 cup heavy cream with Sweet 'N Low® until soft peaks form. Whip chocolate mixture to lighten, about 2 minutes. Fold the whipped cream into the chocolate mixture. Refrigerate for several hours before serving.

Blueberry Mousse

1 lb. plus $1/2$ cup fresh blueberries, washed

3 tablespoons granulated Sweet 'N Low®

$1^1/2$ cups plus $1/2$ cup heavy whipping cream, whipped

$1^1/4$ teaspoons vanilla extract

Serves four – 2.8 carb grams per serving

In a large bowl, crush the blueberries and blend in the Sweet 'N Low.® Fold in $1^1/2$ cups of whipped cream and add the vanilla extract, mixing thoroughly. Divide evenly among 4 individual cups or parfait glasses and chill. Garnish each serving with a dollop of the remaining blueberries and whipped cream.

Crème Hawaii

3 eggs, beaten

2 tablespoons granulated Sweet 'N Low®

$^1/_4$ teaspoon salt

2 cups cream, warmed

1 teaspoon coconut extract

$^1/_2$ teaspoon vanilla extract

$^1/_2$ cup Macadamia nuts, finely chopped

Preheat oven to 350° F.

Serves six – 7.2 carb grams per serving

In a large bowl, thoroughly blend the eggs, Sweet 'N Low® and salt. Gradually add the cream and extracts; then gently fold in the nuts. In a baking dish, at least 2 inches deep, place 6 custard cups. Pour the custard mixture evenly among the custard cups and fill the baking dish with hot water, about 1 inch high. Bake for 1 to $1^1/_2$ hours; then chill in the refrigerator for at least 2 hours before serving.

Lime Sorbet

2 teaspoons lime zest, finely grated

4 cups water

$^1/_4$ teaspoon salt

$^3/_4$ cup lime juice

3 tablespoons granulated Sweet 'N Low®

Serves eight – 5.5 carb grams per serving

In a pot, boil the lime zest and salt in the water for 5 minutes. Allow to cool before adding the lime juice and Sweet 'N Low®; blend thoroughly. Pour the mixture into ice cube trays and freeze. Remove from ice cube trays and break cubes into pieces; serve in parfait or shallow dishes.

Vanilla Ice Cream

6 eggs

24 oz. half and half

$^1/_4$ teaspoon salt

1 tablespoon plus 2 teaspoons vanilla extract

4 teaspoons granulated Sweet 'N Low®

3 tablespoons sugar-free syrup

1 cup whipping cream

Serves eight – 12.3 carb grams per serving

In a bowl, beat the eggs, half and half, salt and vanilla extract. Pour the mixture in a saucepan and heat on a low-medium fire, until the sides of the pan begin to coat with the mixture or the mixture begins to bubble. Pour the mixture in the ice cream maker and add the whipping cream. The ice cream should take approximately 30 minutes to 1 hour depending on the temperature of the mixture and your machine. Once the ice cream begins to harden add the syrup and the Sweet 'N Low.® Let the ice cream finish processing. Serve immediately or freeze for another time.

Optional

Coconut Ice Cream: *coconut extract can be substituted for the 1 tablespoon of vanilla extract.*

Coffee Ice Cream: *add 5 tablespoons concentrated coffee to the mixture.*

Strawberry Ice Cream: *strawberry extract can be substituted for the 1 tablespoon of vanilla extract. For color, a dash of red food coloring may be added, if desired.*

Ted's Chocolate Almond Ice Cream

1 cup roasted almonds, sliced or slivered

$3^{1}/_{2}$ oz. chocolate (60-70% cocoa content), finely chopped

6 eggs

24 oz. half and half

$^{1}/_{4}$ teaspoon butter extract

1 tablespoon plus 2 teaspoons vanilla extract

$^{1}/_{4}$ teaspoon salt

1 cup whipping cream

4 teaspoons granulated Sweet 'N Low®

3 tablespoons sugar-free syrup

Serves eight – 18.5 carb grams per serving

In a bowl, melt the chocolate in the microwave for approximately 15 to 20 seconds or until fully melted. In another bowl, beat the eggs; add the half and half, extracts and salt. Pour the mixture in a saucepan and cook on medium-low heat until the sides of the pan begin to coat with the mixture or until it begins to bubble. Pour the mixture into the ice cream maker; then add the whipping cream. The ice cream should take approximately 30 minutes to 1 hour, depending on your machine, before it begins to harden. Once the ice cream begins to harden, add the Sweet 'N Low,® syrup and almonds. Allow the ice cream to finish processing before serving.

Vanilla Sauce

2 egg yolks

4 teaspoons granulated Sweet 'N Low®

2 cups milk

2 teaspoons vanilla extract

2.0 carb grams per 2 Tablespoons

In a bowl, blend the egg yolks with the Sweet 'N Low.® In a saucepan, scald the milk and gradually add the egg yolk mixture. Return the mixture to the saucepan and stir constantly on medium heat until the sauce coats the back of the spoon. Strain the sauce before adding the vanilla extract. May be served on top of fresh fruit, ice cream or pie.

Chocolate Sauce

$^3/_4$ cup cream

$^1/_2$ teaspoon granulated Sweet 'N Low®

$1^1/_2$ oz. chocolate (60-70% cocoa content), finely chopped

2.3 carb grams per 2 Tablespoons

In a saucepan, bring the cream and Sweet 'N Low® to a boil; then remove from heat. Add the chocolate to the cream. After 1 minute, begin stirring from the center until the chocolate is completely dissolved. May be used to dip strawberries or on top of ice cream.

Praline Sauce

$^1/_2$ cup butter or margarine

$^3/_4$ cup sugar-free maple syrup

$^1/_2$ cup chopped pecans

$^1/_2$ cup chopped walnuts

1 tablespoon vanilla extract

3.4 carb grams per 2 Tablespoons

In a small saucepan, blend the butter or margarine, syrup, nuts and extract. Over medium-high heat, bring the mixture to a boil; then remove immediately. May be served over vanilla ice cream.

Berry Slice

$^1/_2$ cup lemon juice

$^1/_2$ cup fresh blueberries

$^1/_2$ cup fresh raspberries

$^1/_2$ cup diet Slice®

$^1/_2$ cup diet Sprite®

1 cup cream

$1^1/_2$ teaspoons granulated Sweet 'N Low®

Serves four – 9.85 carb grams per serving

In a blender, blend all ingredients until smooth.

Strawberry Cheeseshake

1 cup fresh strawberries

1 cup cream cheese, room temperature

$^1/_2$ cup water

1 teaspoon orange extract

$^1/_2$ teaspoon vanilla extract

$1^1/_2$ teaspoons granulated Sweet 'N Low®

Serves two – 10.8 carb grams per serving

In a blender, blend all ingredients until smooth.

Peachy Banana Ice Cream Shake

$^3/_4$ cup fresh peach slices

1 cup vanilla ice cream (see Index)

$^1/_2$ cup heavy cream

$^1/_2$ cup hot water

$^1/_2$ teaspoon banana extract

Serves four – 13.6 carb grams per serving

In a blender, blend all ingredients until smooth.

Grape Cream Frappé

1 cup fresh seedless grapes

1 cup diet Sprite®

$^{1}/_{2}$ cup vanilla ice cream (see index)

Serves four – 11.7 carb grams per serving

In a blender, blend all ingredients until smooth. Serve over ice.

Maria's Coffee Freeze

$^{1}/_{2}$ cup concentrated coffee

$^{1}/_{2}$ cup heavy whipping cream

2 cups water

1 teaspoon vanilla extract

2 teaspoons granulated Sweet 'N Low®

4 cups ice

Serves four – 2.7 carb grams per serving

In a blender, blend all ingredients until smooth.

index

A

G

H

i

L

M

N

O

R

S

Seafood
Crab

Mussels